MARCIA
CLARK

MARCIA CLARK

CLIFFORD L. LINEDECKER

PINNACLE BOOKS
KENSINGTON PUBLISHING CORP.

PINNACLE BOOKS are published by

Kensington Publishing Corp.
850 Third Avenue
New York, NY 10022

First Printing: April, 1995

Printed in the United States of America

To my cousins, Frank and Barbara Evans, for their consistent support, encouragement, and sense of humor that helps carry me through the dark times.

ACKNOWLEDGMENTS

Many people deserve my thanks for helping pull me through the harried and stressful experience of putting together this book in time to meet an exhaustingly critical deadline.

Thanks are due to my agent Tony Seidl of T. D. Media in New York and to his colleagues there for their efforts on my behalf; to Paul Dinas, my editor at Pinnacle Books, for his continued confidence and support; and to Mike McClay in Los Angeles for his very vital help collecting so much information in such a short time.

Finally, my special thanks go to my wife, Junko, for her tolerance and understanding of the special pressures that must so often be endured by authors and their families.

CONTENTS

Introduction

Marcia Clark was propelled into instant celebrity when she stepped into the spotlight as a lead prosecutor of former-football-superstar-turned-Hollywood-actor O. J. Simpson on twin murder charges.

Caught up in an orgy of publicity, she is getting more attention from the press than President Clinton or the First Lady. Her face has appeared on the front pages and covers of daily newspapers, magazines, and tabloids around the world, and her life, personality, manner of dress, personal grooming habits— even her performance as a mother— have become matters of intense public scrutiny.

Yet, no one has put all the bits and pieces together to reveal the real woman whose abilities and performance are so critical to what is being called "the trial of the century," a high-profile, much analyzed legal proceeding that many professional observers believe will affect the reputation and future of the American legal system.

"You're talking about jurisprudence at stake here," says Harvey Giss, Marcia

Clark's one-time mentor at the Los Angeles County District Attorney's Office.

If Marcia and the State lose, it will appear as if celebrity and loads of money can buy impunity from the law, he has been quoted as observing.

So, just who is Marcia Clark, the bright-eyed, frizzy-haired forty-one-year-old woman on whose narrow shoulders rests so much responsibility?

Among her colleagues with the D.A.'s Office, she is recognized and respected as a tough, capable, hard-hitting prosecutor who has repeatedly proven her ability to deliver victories in difficult homicide cases that are often incredibly complicated. She is a battle-tested veteran of celebrity trials, whose skills and unique dedication to her job are undebatable.

She is unintimidated by the prospect of squaring off in a crowded courtroom before television cameras and millions of spectators around the world, against such high-profile defense attorneys as Robert L. Shapiro, Johnnie Cochran, and F. Lee Bailey.

To some observers she is the aggressive, hard-edged, in-your-face woman seen and heard daily on television, exchanging sarcastic barbs, accusations, and insults, verbal-punch by verbal-punch with the famous defendant's "dream team" of high-paid defense lawyers.

She has been tagged with a variety of labels ranging from "a courtroom tiger," to more politically incorrect terms such as the "O. J. trial pin-up," and a legal eagle "playing the Alexis Carrington role as chief bitch."

It hasn't been easy for Marcia to negotiate the pitfalls that are so unique to professional women. Like her female colleagues in the business of law, she must walk a fine line, balancing her professionalism with her femininity, a task that demands the boldness and sure touch of a circus high wire walker.

Studies have shown that members of juries, both male and female, don't like women lawyers who appear to be too aggressively tough and harshly combative. But no lawyer locked in the fiercely competitive battles of the courtroom can expect to win by behaving like a shrinking violet, either.

Her dazzling courtroom accomplishments, however, represent only one aspect of her multifaceted and intricately fascinating life and personality. She is much more than a successful female assistant district attorney who daily is paraded before the public eye by newspapers and television cameras across the country.

She is a twice-divorced single mother who shops at bargain stores and attends wedding showers with her girlfriends, takes her sons to the park to play, and consumes mystery and suspense novels by the stack.

Marcia Clark is also an intensely private woman, who until she became immersed in the Simpson tragedy, managed to shield her individual identity so closely that even her boss, Los Angeles D.A. Gil Garcetti, eventually confessed he didn't even know if she had a family.

"She is an incredibly hard worker," he says. "She's married to the District Attorney's Office," he told journalists.

But with her emergence as a formidable leading figure in the Super Bowl of murder trials, her privacy has been ripped away. As the most prominently featured member of the prosecution team, she has become locked in a titanic struggle to continue protecting herself and her sons from the personally invasive curiosity of the press and public, while effectively controlling her own destiny.

The O. J. Simpson trial is the most celebrated legal proceeding in recent American history, and it can be properly said that it has developed into two major stories:

One story revolves around the guilt or innocence of the celebrity defendant. Did he indeed ambush his former wife, Nicole, and her friend Ronald Lyle Goldman, and savagely slash them to death in a fit of jealous rage?

The other story deals with even more widely significant questions surrounding the changing roles of women in today's society and their ability to hold down jobs in the outside world while protecting home and hearth and effectively controlling their own destiny.

Already up to her ears in the stressful confrontations and intricately demanding complications of the trial, Marcia Clark has been drawn into the center of a firestorm of debate over the acceptance of women who juggle both an outside job with domestic responsibilities, and the sometimes dreadful price they are expected to pay.

Marcia has wound up waging a war on two fronts.

The outcome of one element in the two-pronged struggle may be critical to the reputation and future of the way Americans look at the effectiveness and fairness of the criminal justice system.

The outcome of the other debate is even more politically charged, yet acutely personal, and strikes at the very core of Marcia's rights, responsibilities, privileges, and future as the mother to her boys.

On a broader scale, the contest could have important implications for other women and the future of their efforts to be accepted in the trades and professions as equals who can hold responsible positions and excel outside the home.

Both stories are still playing out.

Clifford L. Linedecker
April 1995

Prologue

Neighbors responding to an agitated dog whose paws were smeared with blood and barked for hours, led police to a scene of horror that has developed into the most celebrated crime and sensational murder trial in American history.

A few minutes after midnight when authorities responded to a report of a possible burglary at the condominium on South Bundy Drive in the upscale Brentwood area of Los Angeles, they discovered the dead bodies of two people on the walkway just outside the door to the apartment.

The gore-streaked corpse of a petite blond woman was curled up in a pool of blood on its left side with her hands clutched to her breasts. Her head had been nearly severed from her body by a heavy knife or some other sharp object and was still attached to her neck by only a few shreds of skin. She was wearing a black dress and her body was drained almost completely of blood.

The second victim was crumpled on the

concrete walkway at the juncture of two walls. He was an athletically constructed young man, dressed in a brown jacket and bluejeans that were all soiled in ugly smears of blood. His tennis shoes were so completely blood-soaked it was difficult to make out their original color of white. They appeared to be red.

The bright beam from a powerful police flashlight disclosed that one of his eyes was staring and open in a death glaze. His beeper and a blood-stained white envelope containing a pair of women's glasses were lying next to him.

The savagery of the frenzied slashing and stabbing attack, as evidenced by the ghastly condition of the bodies, had the unmistakable look to police of a rage killing. The murders clearly appeared to have occurred during the kind of sloppy, fierce attacks that are committed by someone with close emotional ties to a victim.

Professional hitmen and drug killings are seldom carried out with such ferocity. They are usually cleaner and more efficient, and almost always carried out with guns.

"This appeared to me to be an overkill or a rage killing," Tom Lange, the lead investigator in the case later explained in court.

Investigators quickly identified the bodies. The once strikingly beautiful blonde was Nicole Brown Simpson, the thirty-five-year-old divorced wife of football great, O. J. (Orenthal James) Simpson, who thrilled millions of sports fans when he was a star runningback for the University of Southern California's Trojans, and later cemented his status as a sports superstar with the Buffalo Bills of the American Football Conference's National Football League. She had lived in the apartment with her two children fathered by O. J.

The dog, whose noisy barking led disturbed neighbors to investigate and see what was going on, was Nicole's white Akita. A handsome breed which originated in Japan, the dog's original name was Kato, but that was later changed to Satchmo.

The other victim was Ronald Lyle Goldman, a handsome, six-foot-two-inch, twenty-five-year-old waiter at the Mezzaluna, a restaurant about a ten-minute walk from the townhouse. Colleagues at the restaurant told police he had gone to the apartment after work to return a pair of glasses left at the popular eatery earlier in the evening by Nicole's mother, Juditha Brown.

Veteran investigators Philip Vannatter and Mark Fuhrman of the Los Angeles Police Department were among the first detectives to arrive at the scene. The morning after the slaying, the tall, lanky Fuhrman, was designated by his colleagues to scramble over a wall at O. J.'s posh Rockingham estate a couple of miles from the murder site to check for other possible victims.

In a guest house at the back of the estate, Fuhrman awakened Brian "Kato" Kaelin, an occasional actor with long blond hair who was a friend of both O. J. and his ex-wife. No one was found in the main house.

LAPD Patrolman Robert Riske and his partner were the first lawmen on the murder scene, and cautiously negotiated a path past a trail of bloody shoe prints that continued on to the back entrance before fading away, to take a quick look through the townhouse. He found a letter with O. J.'s name on it. He used the telephone in the kitchen to call his watch commander and advise him that O. J. had a connection of some sort to the case. Riske later explained he didn't use his walkie-talkie because he knew that news reporters listen to police communications on scanners.

"I didn't want to broadcast that there was a possible double homicide involving a celebrity," he remarked. "The media would beat my backup there." The young officer appeared to have been unaware that by using the telephone he might have obscured fingerprints.

He also found two sleeping children, a boy and a girl. After he woke them up, the girl, Sydney, told him their father was O. J. Simpson. Officers drove the youngsters to the police station.

There was no indication that a struggle had occurred inside the townhouse or that it had been ransacked. The television set was on in the master bedroom, and music was playing on the stereo downstairs.

About the only things Riske observed inside the darkened condominium that appeared at all unusual was a cardboard cup of Ben & Jerry's ice-cream that was melting on a bannister, and the tub in the master bath that was filled with water and the room was lighted solely by candles. Nicole was apparently preparing to take a relaxing candlelight bath.

Police Sergeant David Rossi, who was the watch commander that night, secured the murder scene in order to avoid obliterating or contaminating evidence.

Marcia Rachel Clark, a vibrant, intense veteran prosecutor, was the first member of the Los Angeles County District Attorney's Office to show up at the crime scene and at O. J.'s estate. She stayed at the athlete's home about an hour, studying the layout and observing the work of LAPD evidence technicians and other investigators.

Ironically, Marcia came within a few days of missing what would quickly become the biggest, most sensational and personally challenging homicide case of her career and the defining experience of her life.

A few months earlier, after more than a decade of prosecuting homicide cases, including some of the most notorious murders in modern Los Angeles County history, she was promoted and given a substantial raise in pay.

Her bosses, D.A. Gil Garcetti and Deputy D.A. William Hodgman moved her up to a position as Hodgman's special assistant when he took over as Director of the Bureau of Operations. In her new desk job it was her responsibility to supervise the prosecution of career criminals and assign individual cases to other assistant D.A.s. It was a well-deserved promotion that she earned through her diligence, success, and loyal service with the office.

Furthermore, as a single parent, the pay raise, which would boost her annual salary from a bit more than $97,000 well into six figures with the promise of more in the immediate future, was welcome. She had almost reached the limit of the amount of money she could earn in trial work.

There was another apparent advantage as well. The supervisory position was considerably less stressful than assembling and analyzing the mountains of information necessary to prosecute a complicated homicide case, come up with planning strategy, moving on to the demanding requisites of preliminary hearings, and finally, the trial itself.

Throughout her career as an assistant D.A., Marcia had been assigned to tough cases, intricately challenging, make-or-break contests whose outcomes made the difference between imprisonment or freedom, life or death, for some of the most brutal killers in the history of the City of Angels.

It was routine for her to be matched against some of the most skilled and experienced criminal defense attorneys in the business, such as Robert Shapiro, whose reputations and careers depended on their ability to be consistent winners in the courtroom. Trials she was involved in often extended for months, and sometimes dragged on for more than a year.

Marcia was always acutely aware that her preparation and performance could make the difference between removing a savage killer from the streets or releasing him, or her, back into the community. It was sobering knowledge.

Prosecuting homicide cases was exhausting, energy-depleting work that demanded total concentration and commitment. The awesome responsibilities and demands had left too many of her colleagues drained and burned out after only a few years. It seemed to Garcetti that she had earned a respite, and it was time for her to move up to the still important but much less strenuously debilitating supervisory position.

But Marcia missed the stimulation and heady adrenaline rush of pitting herself head-to-head with an opponent in the volatile, emotion-charged arena of the courtroom. A paper-littered desk and stale office work weren't for her. The courtroom was her turf; the place where she felt most comfortable and alive.

She pleaded with her boss for a transfer back to the Special Trials Unit. It was a startling request that, among other things, signalled a significant sacrifice in salary. Nobody with the District Attorney's Office could remember anyone ever doing that before.

But no one working for the LA D.A.'s Office should have been all that shocked by their colleague's self-sacrificing decision. She was a trailblazer; and even if some of her fellow A.D.A.s may have considered her move a step backwards or a step down, Marcia was known as the kind of feisty, decisive individual who didn't hesitate to take bold actions. When she wanted something, she didn't worry or fuss about how she might look to someone else. She went after it.

She was a woman who had paid her dues as an assistant D.A., and her boss agreed to allow her to move back into her old slot in Special Trials as soon as a replacement supervisor could be moved into position.

The transfer came through just three days before the double killing in front of Nicole Simpson's apartment. Shortly before the transfer, Marcia had filed for divorce from her husband of twelve years, Gordon Clark.

In the midst of all the portentous changes that were occurring in her life, Marcia still managed to make time to plan a bridal shower for one of her best friends at work, fellow A.D.A. Lynn Reed (Baragona.) Typical of the time constraints on A.D.A.s who worked in the trial division, there wasn't a lot of time available to the women who planned to participate so they scheduled the celebration for their lunch break on June 13.

At the last moment, Marcia made a quick telephone call to her chum and begged off attending the shower. She had important work to do. The bride-to-be was nonplussed and asked Marcia how she could cancel out, when it was she who had planned the event.

Marcia explained she had to prepare a search warrant. Reed-Baragona was quoted by a journalist months later as saying her friend explained she was working on something that "could end up being kind of big," and promised to fill her in later.

A few days after Marcia's understatement to her colleague, family and friends attended funerals for Nicole Simpson and Ronald Goldman. O. J. attended the rites for his wife with his small son and daughter.

Shortly after the funeral, authorities announced murder charges would be filed against him, and he and his longtime buddy, Al Cowlings led a cordon of police cars on a bizarre freeway chase that was televised to homes across the country. During the sixty-mile dash along a leg of Interstate 405, Cowling stayed at the wheel of his friend's gleaming white Bronco while O. J. sat in the back with the barrel of a gun to his head.

The chase ended in the driveway of the former star athlete's mansion, where he surrendered after a brief period of negotiation. O. J. was placed under arrest and transported to jail to be held under high bail on twin counts of murder.

One of O. J.'s lawyers later hailed Cowlings as a heroic figure who saved his chum's life. O. J. had planned to go to Nicole's grave and commit suicide, but Cowlings talked him out of it, according to superstar criminal defense attorney Robert L. Shapiro.

In the meantime, Marcia not only missed her colleague's wedding shower, but she worked through much of the long Fourth of July weekend in Nicole's condominium apartment, checking it out and getting the lay-of-the-land.

Since joining the D.A.'s staff, meticulous investigations were lynchpins of the hard-driving prosecutor's preparation for cases she handled. The Number Three man in the D.A.'s Office, Hodgman personally selected her as co-prosecutor in the case, and she immediately settled in for a long-drawn-out contest that was to become the fight of her life.

Even though Hodgman was Marcia's immediate superior, and had handled forty murder trials, exactly twice as many cases as she had, she quickly found herself thrust into the spotlight and getting the lion's share of the attention focused on the rapidly expanding prosecution team by the media and the public.

She plunged firmly and unalterably into her task, assuming the State's starring role in an electrifying criminal trial that would make her name and face better known

than fictional lawyers Perry Mason and
Matlock or real-life U. S. Attorney General
Janet Reno.

Chapter One

Marcia Rachel Kleks

Marcia Rachel Kleks was a California girl who enjoyed many of the benefits of spending a large portion of her formative years living in coastal cities of the Golden State.

But she was no "Beach Blanket Bunny," who grew up flirting with handsome blond surfers, playing volleyball, and idly sunbathing on the warm sands of Southern California during her pre-teen and early teenage years.

As the daughter of Abraham I. Kleks, an Israeli immigrant, and Rozlyn Mazur Kleks, a native of New York, she and her only sibling, a brother, were raised in a strictly orthodox Jewish family. Her parents were firm supporters of her father's homeland, Israel.

Closer to home, their political convictions were strongly in line with the positions and programs espoused by liberal Democrats. The couple was politically liberal and religiously conservative.

Abraham Kleks was a chemist and an administrator with the U. S. Food & Drug Administration, and he was frequently transferred. Consequently, the family moved often, and during their tumbleweed travels around the country they settled at various times in Michigan, Texas, Maryland, and Staten Island in New York.

But much of Marcia's childhood and youth was spent in the Northern California area, in fog-drenched communities around the San Francisco Bay. And people who know her today say she is still firmly a Californian, even though there were periods in her life when she lived in other states in the Midwest, South, and the East.

She was born in Berkeley, California, on Monday, August 31, 1953, the same year *TV Guide* began publication, *Playboy* magazine was launched with a daring nude photo of film actress Marilyn Monroe, and the first of Hollywood's ill-fated 3-D films, *Bwana Devil*, was shown.

Her astrological sign is Virgo, the virgin, and her element is earth. Accordingly, the baby girl could be expected to grow up to be intellectual, methodical, placid, and tactless. People who put store in such things as the zodiac and astrological charts, consider Virgos to be nitpickers who are obsessed with detail.

On the rugged east side of the San Francisco—Oakland Bay Bridge, in Alameda County, Berkeley is best known as the center of much of the political radicalism and upheaval that festered on the University of California campus there and split the nation apart during America's involvement in the war in Vietnam.

One of the California communities Marcia's family settled in was Foster City, an upper middle-class San Mateo County suburb of San Francisco. It was a new community on the Bay side of the peninsula at the foot of the San Mateo Toll Bridge.

While she was growing up, other youngsters her age or not much older than she were making San Francisco point central for the Love Generation. Teenage hippies, bikers, druggies, and other assorted longhairs were spilling into the Haight from all over the country, preaching and practicing excess and free love.

But she and her brother were kept busy while all that was going on, bearing down on their studies at school, attending Hebrew classes twice a week, and hitting the books at home. As an adult, her brother became an electrical engineer in Los Angeles. Abraham and Rozlyn Kleks were loving, attentive parents who expected academic excellence from their children.

Marcia was a teenager during America's involvement in the Southeast Asian war. But even though she was intensely socially conscious and shared many of the same high ideals and hopes for the future as her friends, she was no political agitator who frittered away her energies and time by marching in Bay Area anti-war protests or blockading Army recruitment centers.

The slender, doe-eyed girl with the soft shoulder-length dark brown hair, was studious and for a time was so sheltered by her religious parents that when she went out she was watched over by a cautiously solicitous female chaperone who didn't speak English. For years, there were times when she covered her face with a veil.

But neither culture, recreation, nor the formation of long-lasting friendships were neglected in her life. She helped develop poise and confidence with ballet lessons, fussed about clothes, whispered schoolgirl confidences with her chums over boys, and shared heady daydreams with friends about making the world a better place to live.

Like other teenagers, she listened to contemporary music, and especially liked The Doors.

At other times she spent long, wind-blown hours at the rudder of her personal dinghy with a close girlfriend, Rosalyn Dauber, skimming across the choppy waters of the Bay. Thirty years later Roslyn is living and working in the Los Angeles area, where she produces documentary films. One of the films won an Academy Award.

Marcia was still a teenager in 1968 when her father was transferred to a job in New York across the continent from California, and she enrolled as a student at the Susan Wagner High School on Staten Island. Her class was the first to graduate from the newly constructed school.

The Kleks family lived in a house on Queen Street in Meiers Corners during the three years they were on Staten Island. Instead of peering at the sun setting over the Pacific Ocean, she now watched it rise over the Atlantic.

During the summers, she sunbathed for long hours in the back yard of the family's home, relaxing and reading novels. During the school months, however, Marcia was too busy to spend much time lounging around.

She maintained a busy, frenetic schedule. It was a habit that was already deeply ingrained, and would stay with her as an adult. Marcia was a standout student at Susan Wagner High, and impressed her classmates with her quick intelligence, energy, and talent. She did well in all of her classes, had a good relationship with her teachers, and displayed a special fondness for biology.

She also formed close new relationships with schoolmates, threw herself enthusiastically into her studies, and busied herself with extracurricular school affairs. She dated a boy who was much like she was, a free spirit with a strong streak of the cerebral.

Her strong sense of social consciousness was shocked when a wave of racial conflict flared through the school.

She was in tears one day when she approached Harold Boyd, who was black and the senior class president, as he was in the student government office. Marcia told him that she was upset because she couldn't understand why the two of them were able to get along so well together and others couldn't. Marcia left a vivid impression on him, as she did most of her classmates.

Most of the conversations she had with Boyd were philosophical, and he was taken with her quick intelligence and maturity. That didn't mean however, that she was a dull stick-in-the-mud who was so lost in philosophical thought she didn't know how to have a good time. "She was a lot of fun, but never childish," he said recently.

Some of her friends from those years later recalled her as a leader, who was a bit daring, unconventional, and fun to be around. They considered her to be more of a woman-of-the-world than they were, but she was well liked.

According to one of her classmates, Barbara Olsen Benson, in an interview with the *Staten Island Advance,* Marcia could be forward and assertive at times, but she was popular with the boys.

"We had some wild times. I remember she was a flower child and wore dramatic eye makeup," the Richmond, N. Y. woman was quoted as saying. "If Marcia is remembered, it would be for her eyes," she added.

Marcia loved to dance, and she discovered that she also had a flair for acting. She could be quietly reserved or animated and buoyant, and theatrics seemed to come naturally to her. She was a standout member of the high school Drama Club, and appeared in plays. One of her choice roles was a part she played in 1970 in *The Man Who Came To Dinner.*

The long-legged teenager was carried onstage in a sarcophagus and got to dress up in a wispy feather boa, thick shawls with heavy earrings and clogs. Her fellow thespians were impressed with the dramatic flair she showed with a long cigarette holder she was required to flourish in the role.

A friend from those days, Suzanne Grabe Devlin, who became a police lieutenant in Fairfax, Virginia, recalled that Marcia handled the cigarette holder with as much flair backstage as she did onstage. She knew what she was doing.

Lieutenant Devlin especially remembered Marcia for her independence and for her maturity. "When we were fifteen, she was twenty-five. wouldn't be surprised if she became the first woman to be president of the United States," she told an *Advance* reporter.

A few weeks before classes broke for the summer, the *Advance* ran a photograph of Marcia and other members of the cast on the teen page. A policeman's son, Boyd, played one of three leads in the production. Marcia and another boy were the others.

The coach of the Drama Club was just as impressed with Marcia as the teenager's classmates were. Looking back years later, Felicia DeBetta recalled her as an exceptional student. And like Suzanne Devlin, she was struck by the maturity the schoolgirl showed.

"She wasn't a girl, she was a woman," the teacher admiringly told an *Advance* reporter. She said she had often wondered what happened to the vibrant and creative young woman.

Although Marcia was one of the most popular students at the school, she wasn't able to share in any of the graduation festivities with fellow members of the Class of '71. Her father was transferred again, and his family was once more dragged across the country.

She left Susan Wagner High in January, and her diploma was mailed to her. Despite her accomplishments and popularity, her photograph wasn't even included in the high school yearbook.

Her drama coach, Boyd, and others figured that she would likely pursue a career as an actress.

By late summer of 1972 she was back in her home state, enrolled as a political science major at the University of California Los Angeles. William Hodgman, who would later become Marcia's boss and is the same age as she, was one of her classmates. Like Marcia, he graduated four years after enrollment with a degree in political science.

At UCLA, Marcia continued her work in theatre, and continued to seriously consider some day taking up professional acting. She also followed up on her childhood experience with ballet by launching into serious study of dance. For a while she toured with a professional dance troupe.

But the life of the pretty, talented coed was about to take a far different direction from either professional dancing or acting.

Chapter Two

Life in the Fast Lane

Surrounded by the invigorating freedom and challenges of campus life, she was far removed from the earlier years as a sheltered daughter whose parents' caution led her to wear a veil and travel with a chaperone. College is an exciting, stimulating experience, a time when the young traditionally test their wings, develop new relationships and begin to throw off parental restrictions and strike out on their own. Marcia was no exception.

It was while the enthusiastic, studious young woman was at UCLA that she met Gabriel Horowitz.

Family members and friends of the athletically built six-foot, two-inch, curly-haired Israeli called him "Gaby." He was bold and flamboyant and decked himself out in perfectly tailored casual suits, with a Rolex watch and flashy gold jewelry that included an expensive bracelet and a chain and pendant he wore around his neck. He even wore the jewelry when he went to the beach.

Gaby was intelligent, with a quick, facile

mind and was movie-star handsome. He
was absolutely charming when he wished
to be, and he had a reputation among
some of his acquaintances as a bit of a
rascal. He exhibited the sure confidence
that came with being a military veteran
who had served in his country's Air Force
during the bloody Arab-Israeli Six-Day
War in June, 1967. He loved guns and ac-
quired a modest collection of weapons,
which he kept in his home and fired often
at local shooting ranges.

Gaby made an excellent living for himself
as a professional backgammon player in the
waning years of the 1970s after the political
and social turbulence of the early part of
the decade had quieted down. He was an
expert whose wizard-like ability to concentrate on the mind-taxing game was belied
by his theatrical flair. He often glided into
one of the luxurious clubs where games and
tournaments were played, wearing a long,
sweeping cloak.

Marcia was bowled over by the dashing
globe-trotting lady-killer and boldly adventurous playboy. In 1973 she moved into a
sunny Hollywood apartment on Palmero
Camino with him and began a new phase
of her life that was as colorful and shock-
ingly tempestuous as an episode of *Dy-
nasty*.

Marcia had always kept busy, but as the

exciting gambler's live-in girlfriend, there were hardly enough hours in her life to keep up with her crammed schedule of activities.

Marcia shuttled between school, their home, and exclusive private clubs and public casinos in the Americas and Europe where Gaby's apparent talents, skills, and luck as a backgammon hustler enabled him to earn a fortune. Some other players who knew him in those days say his total winnings amounted to more than $1 million.

Backgammon is an old game that pits two players against each other with fifteen-round pieces each, which they move according to the throw of dice. A variation of the game called acey-deucey is especially popular with sailors, and is a recreational mainstay in Navy barracks and aboard ships.

Players on the backgammon circuit worked by Marcia's sweetheart often squared off in exhausting tournaments that could last for several hours or even days. And the stakes played for were a far cry from a sailor's pay.

Small fortunes exchanged hands while Gaby played with some of the best professionals and best amateurs in the world. John Wayne and Lucille Ball were two of the better known celebrities who pitted their abilities at the backgammon board against those of the devil-may-care Israeli.

The Duke reportedly sometimes lost thousands of dollars to him in a single afternoon. But the late cowboy star's films and other activities had made him so wealthy, he wasn't bothered by the losses. Lucy also left the backgammon tables with her purse thousands of dollars lighter after pitting her skills against Gaby's phenomenal winning ways. Gaby won a tournament she sponsored and walked off with a handsome loving cup, as well as a pile of money.

Marcia frequently accompanied Gaby, and tried her own hand at backgammon. She learned to play well, but never developed the same obsession with the game that he did. Sometimes, with her dark curly hair parted in the middle and flowing over her shoulders, she perched unobtrusively on a chair next to him during one of the marathon backgammon sessions, quietly rooting for him and watching him play. She was usually lugging a load of textbooks and other reading matter along with her, however, which she pored over in another room while he played.

Marcia also jetted to Europe and the Caribbean with him while he played in casinos at Monte Carlo, San Juan, and at other exotic hot spots that were on the backgammon circuit. And she was nearby, hovering in the background when he played at private clubs such as Pips in Los Angeles, the ultra-exclusive Cavendish in Beverly Hills a few blocks from the fabled Sunset Strip, and other locations frequented by Hollywood stars, athletes, and the big money crowd.

Pips was the backgammon headquarters in those days for a glittering array of celebrities, including Hugh Hefner, Dean Martin, and actors and former football greats Jim Brown— and O. J. Simpson. They all played the intriguing board game.

During the early 1970s, there was a backgammon craze, and the game was wildly popular. Most players participated for recreational purposes, as a respite from the demands and stresses of their jobs and daily lives. But there was a huge amount of money to be made in the game and Gaby was determined to get his share.

If some of his associates and fellow players from those years are to be believed, Gaby's extraordinary talents and charismatic personality enabled him to display such aplomb and win so consistently at the backgammon boards.

As a result, he was not welcomed at some of the top backgammon playing sites in Greater Los Angeles. Unable to move as freely as he had in the past, he grew bitter and did not react cavalierly to losing as he had before.

In a reference to a world champion chess player also known for his temperamental outbursts, one acquaintance described Gaby as the Bobby Fisher of backgammon. According to one example cited by a onetime backgammon promoter during an interview for the *Enquirer*, after Gaby had demanded total silence from spectators, a man in the gallery became excited at the play and made a noise. Gaby screamed at him that he was barred. When someone else pointed out that the offender was a deaf mute, Gaby snatched up a piece of paper and angrily scratched a note on it, then shoved it at the man.

"You are barred from watching this game," the note advised.

According to other reports, Gaby's explosive temper was sometimes turned on Marcia. One neighbor who knew the couple when they were living in the same sunny apartment complex on Palmero Camino in Hollywood told of listening to them screaming furiously at each other in Hebrew.

During the two years they shared a home at the Palmero Camino apartments, Marcia moved in and out at least four times. The couple would face off in one of their ferocious, screaming quarrels and she would leave and move in temporarily with a girl-friend, according to the reports. After a day or two, a week, or a month, she would move back into the apartment and everything would begin all over again.

Sidney Jackson, a former director of the American Backgammon Players Association and his wife, Donna, told a reporter they once personally observed an example of Gaby's anger when he lost his temper while preparations were being made for a tournament. Marcia was reportedly grous-ing that she wanted to go home when he swept up a chair and hurled it at her. The chair slammed harmlessly against a wall, but it hit so hard that it shattered.

Although Marcia later denied that the outrageous chair tossing incident occurred, Jackson said fifty people witnessed the outburst.

The former manager of the Camino Palermo apartments said it was common knowledge among residents there that Gaby and Marcia fought often— and loudly.

Marcia's onetime neighbor recalled a night when she was accompanying them on a drive to the Cavendish and they tan-gled in one of their ferocious quarrels. Gaby became so enraged that he whipped the steering wheel around and jammed the brakes so suddenly he nearly caused the car to crash, the woman said. The couple continued screeching at each other for several minutes after the near accident, before he finally calmed down and resumed driving, she added.

Despite the reputed troubles, or perhaps because of it, the relationship not only survived, but flourished. If it was true that Gaby had some faults that may have distressed her, Marcia seemed to focus on his better qualities. He could be tenderly attentive and sensitively affectionate when things were going his way and he was in a good mood. The audacious gambler was excitingly romantic, and had opened an entire world of adventure and high living for her.

Shortly after they moved out of the Hollywood apartment, Marcia and Gaby were married. It was November 6, 1976. His mother, Clara, was a dressmaker, and she created the white linen gown that Marcia wore for the ceremony. The older woman also gave her the diamond for the engagement ring.

The newlyweds posed together for snapshots at a tony vacation spa in Palm Springs.

In 1977 Marcia pulled on a light sweater, covered her long slender legs with a pair of bluejeans and drove southeast along the Santa Ana Freeway to Disneyland at Anaheim with Gaby. His mother, Clara, went along with the couple on the outing.

According to Clara, her daughter-in-law's hair was becoming so thin at that time that Marcia had begun wearing a wig.

Gaby's best friend, Bruce Roman, a lanky Los Angeles accountant and minister in the Church of Scientology, and his girlfriend, sometimes vacationed with the young couple. Roman and his sweetheart joined them for a fling in Mexico in 1978. During the day they lolled on sun-drenched beaches, and evenings they dined and danced the night away in palm-tree-lined resorts.

Roman was also an excellent backgammon player, as well as a minister in the Church of Scientology which has attracted thousands of followers including such internationally known celebrities as Tom Cruise, John Travolta, and Lisa Marie Presley.

Around the time the couples vacationed together in Mexico, Gaby paid for Marcia to have a nose job. She was already a beautiful young woman, with long legs, a trim figure, lovely long dark hair, and expressive intelligent eyes. But she thought her nose was too big.

After the operation, she had a new nose, smaller and bobbed slightly upward at the tip revealing a more prominent look at her nostrils. The surgery was expensive, but Gaby was keeping busy at the backgammon tables and making a lot of money.

Marcia was marking up other important

changes in her life as well, that had nothing to do with her physical appearance but
a lot to do with her abilities and future
independence. Abandoning the idea of
making a life for herself as a professional
dancer, she formed new career plans that
were unrelated to the entertainment business or to professional gambling. She set
her sights on becoming a lawyer.

After she graduated from UCLA with a
political science degree, she entered law
school. Marcia attended classes at the
Southwestern University School of Law in
Los Angeles. Gaby reportedly footed the
bill and paid for her expenses.

Gaby's graduation present to her after
she completed law school and passed her
California bar examination in 1979 was a
two-week tour of Europe.

The whirlwind European holiday was
the star-crossed couple's last hurrah, however. Marcia wasn't the same wide-eyed romantic and dependent girl who had moved
into the Camino Palmero apartments with
Gaby more than six years earlier. She had
become a confident, independent woman
who wanted more than being a shadow to
her temperamental, difficult husband.

Marcia was nearing thirty, and she'd
been raised to expect more from life than
beaches and carousels, teeth-rattling quarrels, and backgammon. It would be diffi-

cult to imagine settling down with the unpredictable gambler.

A year later Marcia walked out of her marriage on July 15, 1980. They had been together almost seven years.

A week after Marcia moved out, through her attorney, she filed in the Los Angeles County Superior Court for a divorce from her husband. The catch-all phrase, "irreconcilable differences," was cited as grounds.

Sanford D. Gilbert was named on the divorce petition as her attorney. In later documents, Howard R. Price, another family law attorney with offices at the same West Pico Boulevard address in Los Angeles was listed as her lawyer. Gaby was served with the divorce papers at his home on South Crescent Heights Boulevard, and did not oppose the divorce action in court.

While waiting for the divorce to be finalized, she tried her hand for awhile at waitress jobs. She dressed in off-the-rack clothes, dresses, blouses, and pants she bought at discount stores, and occasionally in items borrowed from friends. The glory days when Gaby paid her bills with his backgammon winnings were over, and she reportedly held down jobs at area restaurants including Lawry's Prime Ribs and a Hamburger Hamlet.

Chapter Three

Marriage, Motherhood, and Divorce

Marcia drove down the California coast near San Ysidro a few minutes south of San Diego, crossed the U. S. border into Mexico to get a quickie Tijuana divorce.

Less than a month later, on October 7, 1980, she was married in Los Angeles to Gordon Tolls Clark. She used her maiden name, Marcia Kleks, on the marriage license, which the couple obtained on the same day they tied the knot.

The bridegroom was a computer expert and executive with the Church of Scientology, who lived in Hollywood.

Ironically, the ceremony was conducted in Marcia's home on North Kings Road in Los Angeles by Gaby's best friend, Bruce Roman. The lanky Los Angeles orthodontist was a lay minister with the controversial church.

While Marcia was getting married for the second time, her American divorce was still making its laborious way through the Los Angeles court and wasn't finalized until almost four months later, on February 2,

1981. As part of the decree, her maiden name, Kleks, was restored.

Gordon and Gaby were about as different as two men could be. Unlike the flamboyant, emotional Israeli gambler, Gordon was a quiet computer wizard from Texas. His father, W. E. Clark, came from Wyoming; his mother, Lynn, hailed from California. Five years younger than Marcia, he was quiet, sober, stable and dedicated to his ministry in Scientology.

Marcia was different as well. Well-traveled and used to the fast track of a gambler's life, she'd become an outgoing young woman, focused on her future profession, confident about tackling life head on.

It seemed like a good match, destined to form the basis of a solid, loving and constructive relationship that Marcia could depend on.

Now that her domestic life was back on track, Marcia wasted no time in using her legal talents. She landed a job with Brodey and Price. It was one of the top law firms specializing in criminal defense in greater Los Angeles, and she was hired under her maiden name, Marcia Kleks.

On the home front the marriage was proceeding on a strong, steady course. Marcia's union with Gordon had neither the flash nor the dashing elegance she had known with his predecessor, but it enabled her to concentrate on her life and future plans.

In 1989, after the couple had been together eight years, Marcia gave birth to their first child. They named the healthy little boy Travis. It was a name that had glorious historical roots in his father's home state, where Colonel William Barret Travis commanded the defenders of the Alamo before falling with Davy Crocket, Jim Bowie, and other heroes to overwhelming Mexican forces.

About the same time the couple were celebrating the birth of their son, they learned the tragic news that Gaby had been shot and was in a coma. Bruce Roman, Gaby's best friend and the lay minister who had married Marcia and Gordon, was the shooter.

Roman was taken into custody and briefly held on suspicion of attempted murder. But he was released after investigation backed up his story that the shooting was accidental and occurred as the two gun collector pals were inspecting a holstered Colt .45. He was quickly cleared of any criminal intent, and the shooting was officially ruled to have been an accident.

Gaby eventually came out of the coma, but fragments of the bullet were still lodged in his brain and he was left wheelchair bound and unable to talk. He became totally dependent on his aged mother for his care. It was a dreadful development for the onetime highroller.

For awhile, she cared for Gaby at their home in Palm Springs. Eventually however, she took him back to Israel and mother and son settled in Tel Aviv.

A little more than two years after Travis's birth, Marcia and her computer engineer husband became the parents of Trevor, their second son. Marcia and Gordon worked at full-time jobs and by that time could afford to hire a live-in housekeeper to help with the boys. But they were both attentive parents. Travis and Trevor were showered with love, and well cared for. Hugs and kisses were never in short supply where the boys were concerned.

But the time was rapidly approaching when serious cracks and chinks in the relationship between their parents began to eat away at the marriage.

By late 1993 tensions and strains similar to those that have shattered so many American families caught up with the Clarks. Two-career marriages, personal growth, the pressures of parenthood; whatever combination of differences and stresses may have been ultimately responsible, by late 1993 their troubles culminated in a split.

Early in the new year, Gordon moved out of the family home. Six months later,

Marcia made the break-up official. On June 9, 1994, she filed in Los Angeles Superior Court for divorce from her husband of nearly thirteen years.

Chapter Four

Attorney for the Defense

Being a junior attorney at Brodey and Price was more a matter of hard work, long hours, and elbow grease than glamour.

Like almost any young lawyer, before Marcia could even begin to realize any dreams she might have of becoming a big-time defense attorney, she had dues to pay.

She was put to work learning and dealing with the basics of the business, busying herself with the mind-numbing mounds of paperwork, briefs, motions, writs, bail requests, depositions, and all the other minutia that goes with the territory.

There were incessant telephone calls, interviews to conduct, and conferences to attend. It wasn't unusual for her to be at her desk, burning the midnight oil and littering an ash tray with cigarette butts, long after most Angelenos had left their offices and other workplaces and were already jamming the streets and highways in their homebound vehicles.

Nor was it unusual when she finally walked through the door at home to greet her husband and boys for her to be lugging her briefcase, heavy with a jumble of paperwork to deal with after dinner was over and the children had been bathed and put to bed.

The work was exciting and stimulating, nevertheless. She was respected by her colleagues, and learning every day. There was always something new to deal with, another knotty problem to work out, more information to soak up and assimilate. Her work must have seemed, for a while, to offer everything she could have hoped for in her professional life.

The junior attorney cut her legal teeth helping more experienced colleagues on several cases before she was instructed to draft a brief asking a judge to dismiss charges of attempted murder against a leader of the violently radical Black Guerrilla Family.

James "Doc" Holiday was accused of luring a woman into a car and stabbing her numerous times before leaving her for dead.

Marcia was working on the document at home when she became so disgusted with herself that she told her husband she couldn't continue. She knew the government's evidence was perilously shallow, and figured there was almost no chance the motion would be denied.

According to her later recollection however, Gordon told her to go ahead and complete the brief. They had rent to pay.

Marcia was right about the case and the court's response to her brief. The judge threw the case out for lack of evidence, and she was horrified at the key role her efforts and skills played in winning the dismissal.

Her success at presenting the client's case in the brief, represented the kiss-of-death for her fledgling career as a defense attorney. The young lawyer was caught in the middle of a personal crisis. She had a decision to make about her future that all attorneys attracted to criminal law must sometime face.

How can they justify representing and helping to return killers, stick-up men, dope dealers, baby beaters, and pedophiles to the streets, then return with a clear conscience to their own families in some secure suburb just as if their hands were clean? How in the world can they ask a judge or jury to exonerate or show mercy for a drive-by shooter, a terrorist, or an arsonist who has firebombed a church or killed scores of people after setting fire to a crowded nightclub?

After spending roughly two years with Brodey and Price, she reportedly had a serious talk with her boss about her reaction and how badly she felt about figuring so prominently in the decision that returned Holiday back onto the streets. Her boss advised her she was probably on the wrong side. She should be working for the Los Angeles County District Attorney.

A few days later, Marcia sat down with then Los Angeles County D.A. John Van de Kamp and soberly informed him that it was up to him whether or not she practiced the profession she was trained for.

She couldn't do criminal defense work, and had no desire to spend the rest of her working life handling divorces, personal injury lawsuits, or litigating other civil matters. She had her heart and mind set on becoming a prosecutor. Marcia was determined to represent victims and to guard the people's rights and safety. Someone else could represent the criminals.

Van de Kamp was impressed. He gave her the job that would transform her life forever. She became an Assistant District Attorney.

Chapter Five

Public Prosecutor

In 1981 when Marcia was assigned to work as one of only two A.D.A.s at the courthouse in Culver City, she broke into the job prosecuting a grisly procession of homicide cases.

A community of about 40,000, Culver City lies just west of the city of Los Angeles and below the crook of the crossing of the Santa Monica and San Diego Freeways.

There was no time for Marcia to gradually work her way up to the most serious criminal cases adjudicated at the Culver City courthouse, while sharpening her skills on defendants accused of even slightly less horrendous offenses.

She was put right to work specializing in murder. The new A.D.A. was plunged head-over-high-heels into the maelstrom; socked smack in the middle of all that's nasty about life and death in America's big cities.

Street predators; the shooters, gang-bangers, homicidal rapists, urban terrorists, rioters, dope-crazed madmen, and other assorted killers became as familiar and well-known to her as next-door neighbors or local mail carriers are to most other people.

Marcia learned first hand about the savage brutality and the horror of human suffering.

She mastered her trade on the job. She learned the ins and outs of preparing a case, selecting a jury, presenting evidence, and of how a judge controls a courtroom, including little tricks for enforcing discipline among the attorneys.

She had a phenomenal talent for getting the army of people whose cooperation is so necessary to building a rock-solid case and successfully prosecuting it, to help her out. She seemed to have a natural ability to marshall the support of the witnesses, police, evidentiary experts, and legal egg-heads and to use their information and knowledge to the best advantage.

She was meticulous and thorough about details, and her insistence on covering, and sometimes recovering all the bases, paid off with convictions. She did everything she could to build an airtight case before going in front of a judge and jury.

Once when she was working on a particularly difficult double murder involving defendants who were Russian nationals, she sent police and forensic technicians back to the scene of the slaying to look for fingerprints on an item that wasn't previously checked.

The crime-scene technicians obtained the fingerprints, and they wound up as one of the keys to the convictions she won months later. L. A. County Sheriff's Sgt. Dirk Edmundson was one of the homicide detectives who worked with her, and later said he was impressed with the way she was constantly thinking about and building her case.

Marcia appeared to have an instinctive insight into complex issues and the mysteries of such important forensic matters as ballistics, and of serology and its related science, DNA.

Her phenomenal ability was by no means all due to instinct, however. Preparation was a key to much of her success. She barely settled down in her cubicle office at the courthouse before she began putting down a card index file. The information on the cards was taken from reports of appellate court decisions, then trimmed down until they contained only the most pertinent points.

They were a quick and easy reference, but over the years she compiled box after box until she finally quit adding to the files following Trevor's birth. Maintaining the meticulously kept card files was typical of her approach to her job. Every detail concerned with putting a case together and successfully prosecuting it was important to her.

She favored high heels and dark blue or black business suits with short skirts for her courtroom apparel, and wore a watch and a bit of other jewelry including earrings. Opponents who knew her reputation however, were aware that it would have been a mistake of enormous proportions to be misled by believing the length of her skirts or the click of high heels that signalled her femininity meant she could be bullied or intimidated in court.

When she was locked in one of the deadly serious episodes of courtroom combat, she was all business, a thoroughly pragmatic and relentlessly professional prosecutor. Her large, expressive eyes flashed with emotion when she crossed verbal swords with a courtroom antagonist or sought to get a particularly salient point across. She has a tendency to lean her shoulders forward, with her chin out and her neck extended toward the offending lawyer or witness.

The courtroom is her home turf. She is at ease, comfortable and confident there, and it is where she fights fierce battles. A good scrap with an accomplished legal adversary seems to make her think faster, and with even more cutting clarity than ever. She knows how to take apart a specious argument as cleanly and efficiently as an experienced pathologist slices through a cold corpse with a scalpel. She peels back the skin with her incisive mind, and exposes any cancer or rot that might be festering inside her opponent's arguments.

Sgt. Edmundson recalled in a report by the *Los Angeles Times* that when Marcia was getting ready to work on the double-murder prosecution of the Russians, he was reminded of the adrenaline rush that comes before a big sports event. She had a "hungry look," he said.

From the beginning, she demonstrated that she was a person who could think on her feet and cut through the legalistic hocus-pocus thrown up by courtroom antagonists or expert witnesses testifying on anything ranging from such ploddingly dull matters as the whorls and grooves in fingerprints, to the intellectual musings and subjective opinions of psychiatry.

That's a quality that is a prerequisite for a good trial attorney. In the unforgiving crucible of the courtroom, an incisive, quick mind and sharp tongue can make the difference between winning and losing.

She can be an articulate and spell-binding orator, with the ability to rivet a jury's attention with loquaciously convincing opening statements and summations. Her cross-examinations resonate with emotion, and can be as harshly brutal and startlingly graphic as blood pumping on a sidewalk. She loved her job. It made her come vibrantly alive.

Frequently, after a taxing day of dealing with scumbags and gasbags in the courtroom, she would stop off at one of the local watering holes near her office with another A.D.A. or a couple of the cops she was working with on a case. There, among the blue tobacco haze and clink of glasses, they would unwind and celebrate a hard-fought victory. Or, if the trial was still underway, they would pick apart the defense case piece-by-piece, or scheme and map the next day's strategy.

Marcia demonstrated an impressive ability at those gatherings to keep up with her companions in salty language and good cheer. And when someone mentioned a good point she had scored, or a defense misstep, Marcia's delighted laughter would ring out over the buzz of conversation around them.

After awhile she might pick out a cue, chalk it up, and test her skill against one of her pals on a pool table. She is a formidable pool shooter, and just as she does in court, she plays to win.

There were times at work when she would

be faced with an option of getting together with the defense attorney on a case to discuss and consider the possibilities of avoiding the time and expense of a trial by working out an agreement for the defendant to plead guilty to a lesser charge.

Plea bargaining is a necessary evil in the criminal courts system, and at best it has the effect of administering justice in an economic manner. At its worst, it can permit a prosecutor without the confidence or the will to obtain a conviction on the most serious charges possible— or the most appropriate, justified serious charges— to take the easy way out by allowing the defendant to cop a plea.

The tough young prosecutor at Culver City, didn't build her formidable reputation by making a habit of taking the most convenient options, or by exhibiting a readiness to agree to wrist-slap justice. She was typically assigned some of the most confusing and convoluted cases on the calendar. And the people she prosecuted were some of the worst that the mean streets of Los Angeles had to offer. Murder defendants learned that when she was involved they should be prepared to watch her fight for long prison sentences— at the very least. She was a prosecutor who behaved as if she believed in punishment that fit the crime.

She quickly developed a reputation for uncompromising toughness when the situation called for it, but that was one of the very qualities that earned her such respect. A few courtroom wags took to referring to her as "Maximum Marcia."

Many times Marcia would be in one courtroom trying a case, and her colleague, Diane Vezzani would be examining witnesses or addressing a judge and jury in another courtroom a few feet away. The two A.D.A.s became good friends. They were handy sounding boards for each other, and their friendship extended both inside and outside the courthouse. They had much in common.

A close friend who shared similar responsibilities and a similar workload at the courthouse in Culver City was a handy advantage to have. The odds for a young attorney hoping to survive the daunting obstacles and become a successful big city prosecutor are awesome. The courtroom is a pressure cooker where fledgling prosecutors are pushed off the pier or tossed out of the boat and left to sink or swim. There is no middle ground. No one floats.

A.D.A.s get ulcers, have stress attacks, smoke too much, drink too much, and their marriages break up. Not all, of course, fall prey to those ills, but a large number of them do. Others work for a few years, soak up valuable experience at the taxpayers expense, then leave to join private law firms or strike out on their own as high-paid criminal defense attorneys. Consequently, when they take a seat at the defense table, they know all about how prosecutors work—because they've been there.

A top-flight Los Angeles criminal defense lawyer once described the prosecutor's office as a shallow reef stocked with minnows and bait fish that were just beginning to mature. After awhile they could be expected to be seriously thinned out by the hungry tiger sharks and barracuda cruising in from the deep water of big-time criminal defense law firms to feed.

The defense lawyers Marcia came up against her in court quickly learned to respect her. Barry Levin, a top-notch attorney with the city's criminal defense bar talked admiringly of her to the press even though he lost a hard-fought murder case to her that extended twenty months.

Levin described her as tough, but fair, and a courtroom opponent who couldn't be intimidated. He knew what he was talking about because he had tried many times to intimidate her and failed, he admitted. She is good at every phase of trial work.

Chapter Six

Trial by Media:
The James Hawkins Case

When Marcia first met Harvey Giss, he was a crusty veteran who was considered the District Attorney's top gun, the man to see whenever there was a tough or high-profile homicide case to prosecute.

Harvey was the best. He was just the kind of prosecutor the District Attorney needed for a demanding case involving a local folk hero with a flawed character like James Hawkins.

Even a District Attorney's Office super-star like Giss needed help with a case as mentally trying, time demanding, and politically sensitive as the Hawkins trial was shaping up to be. So he selected Marcia Clark as his co-counsel.

The choice of Marcia to work with the highly vaunted veteran, especially on such a fully equal partnership basis, was an incredibly exciting feather in the cap for the hard-driving young prosecutor.

It was recognition by her peers that she was respected on the highest levels of the District Attorney's Office as a thoroughly competent professional who could be counted on when the chips were down. And the chips really were down in the Hawkins case.

For awhile, Hawkins was being hailed in Los Angeles and around the country as a Black Bernie Goetz from the West Coast, a hard-working, mind-your-own-business type of citizen who finally got fed up with criminals taking over the streets and meted out a bitter dose of vigilante justice.

The media loved him, and briefly he may have been one of the most popular men in the United States. To some, he was a reincarnation of Bernie Goetz, the skinny, white, towheaded former mugging victim who was widely hailed as a true American hero after blazing away with a pistol at several young men whom he believed were threatening him on a New York subway.

To others, Hawkins was a real-life philosophical twin to the one-time mild-mannered architect played by Charles Bronson in the popular series of *Death Wish* films, who exploded into violence after his wife and daughter were gang raped by thugs and his wife died.

Most importantly of all, Hawkins was seen as a black man in Watts who stood up and said, "Enough is enough"—then illustrated his frustration and outrage by shooting one of the reputed bad guys. The anger and frustrations of law-abiding citizens over the flaws, escape hatches, and inadequacies of the criminal justice system boiled over in an outpouring of sympathy and admiration for the plucky street-corner shooter.

Watts badly needed exactly the kind of courageous, hard-hitting local heroes like Hawkins appeared to be.

If any neighborhood in Los Angeles has become synonymous in the public mind with menace and runaway violence, it's the sprawling clutter of private homes and housing projects known as Watts that lies several miles southeast of the central city area. Watts is the home of vicious drug gangs who blow each other to bits and anyone else who happens to be in the way, with rapid-firing shotguns known as street sweepers.

Hawkins worked at his father's mom-and-pop grocery store, when his name first appeared in the headlines. He shot a street gang member, whom he claimed was picking on a woman and her five children on the street in front of the store and the gun was discharged by accident.

Nineteen-year-old Anttwon Thomas died in the September 1983 shooting, and Hawkins, his father, and other members of the family immediately found themselves and their grocery store at the center of a vortex of violence. The store was fire-bombed.

News stories flashed around the country about the family's courageous stand against the round of attacks launched by the dead youth's vengeance-seeking gang friends. Longtime Los Angeles Mayor Tom Bradley, a former police officer and city councilman, led the outpouring of public praise for Hawkins and his beleaguered family.

People who were fed up with street thugs and revolving-door justice that permits brutal career criminals to skip in and out of police precinct stations and courts almost faster than law enforcement agencies can process the paperwork, cheered the middle-class heroics of Hawkins and his family.

Months after Hawkins was first hailed as a hero, Giss and other investigators dug out the real facts behind the feud between the Watts family and the street gang. The homicidal brush-up turned out not to be a soul-stirring story of vigilante justice after all.

Hawkins and Thomas were members of rival street gangs. And the grocer's son didn't dash out of the store to rescue the neighbor and her children. He was just one more Los Angeles gang banger, and he shot Thomas at least a half hour after the woman's sidewalk confrontation with the teenager. The inspiring urban fairytale dissolved and soured into just another dreary nightmare incident of violence in the slums.

Hawkins was arrested for the Thomas slaying, amid cries of outrage from supporters who made themselves heard not only in his home neighborhood of Watts, but elsewhere in Los Angeles and throughout the United States.

The outcry became worse when he was charged with additional twin counts of murder for two other killings that had nothing to do with the street corner shooting of the nineteen-year-old. It was a cold-blooded double execution-style slaying and robbery that may have been tied to a territorial dispute over drug dealing and occurred almost a year after Thomas was gunned down. Hawkins was exposed as a menacing street thug, a thoroughly rotten character who was one of the last people imaginable deserving of hero worship or admiration.

Hawkins and a co-defendant were accused of killing reputed drug rivals Roger Grand and Larry Turner on June 18, 1984, while he was free on bail for the fatal Thomas shooting. Turner's body was discovered bound and gagged at his home in South Los Angeles. Grant's corpse was dumped along an area roadway. Both men were shot several times.

The co-defendant was a twenty-nine-year-old convicted murderer who was free on parole when the slayings were carried out.

For awhile Hawkins' arrest on the shocking new charges was an exceedingly unpopular development with many people in Watts who didn't want to give up on their hero.

Whispered threats of another riot were bandied around here and there in the neighborhood, before the Watts grocer's son who was once widely hailed as a hero, was convicted of manslaughter in the Thomas shooting. He was sentenced to a twenty-eight year prison term.

Giss realized however that prosecution for the double-slaying of Turner and Grant was shaping up as one of those gruelling marathon contests that could run on for months. Preparation of sophisticated scientific evidence and the testimony of expert witnesses were expected to play a large role in presentation of the State's case.

He needed help from someone he could trust to do the job efficiently and correctly, and whom he respected as his professional equal. Marcia had forged a reputation for herself as a prosecutor who was always prepared, was a devastating counter-puncher in the courtroom, and was especially skilled at building airtight cases through the testimony and other assistance of police, legal scholars, and evidentiary experts.

Giss explained to Marcia, who had been promoted to Deputy District Attorney, how he felt about his demand for excellence from colleagues he teamed up with, and that she fit the bill. They would split responsibilities for the proceeding on an equal basis as well, he said. An invitation to work with the highly respected veteran prosecutor was a thrilling opportunity for her.

One of Marcia's primary obligations in the case was handling ballistics. Ballistics deals with such important subjects as the grooves inside gun barrels, the individualistic markings they leave on bullets when they're fired, the stipling and residue emitted by the explosion of the gunpowder and other related matters that can play a vital role in police investigations and in the courtroom. It is one of the most challenging of the forensic sciences.

Marshalling the information, evidence, and exhibits relating to ballistics was one of the most difficult aspects of the case, among all the other myriad tasks involved in trial preparation. One of the main reasons for that, was that the prosecutors didn't have the weapon used in the execution shootings of the two reputed drug dealers.

Consequently, it appeared the prosecution would be faced with going to trial and attempting to sway a jury with less dramatic and conclusive evidence about such things as the one-of-a-kind patterns of grooves left by the inside of gun barrels on bullets as they're fired, and other esoterics dealing with ammunition and firearms during the portions of the trial devoted to ballistics.

That could be challenging enough in any homicide case, but the task ahead of the determined prosecutors was especially daunting because they planned to ask for the death penalty. A jury composed of average men and women could be expected to look a bit harder and closer at evidence if a man's life depended on their conclusions.

A few days before the beginning of the trial, the prosecutors had put together a far from airtight case, and they were facing a formidably capable criminal defense team. Barry Levin and Richard Ross, who shared defense responsibilities, were top-notch trial lawyers, who were experienced and knew their way around a courtroom. They knew how to prepare and present a strong case, and could be counted on to take full advantage of the prosecution's inability to produce the weapon used in the

shootings. The gun was a key factor in the
case, and the prosecution didn't have it.

Giss and Marcia were preparing to start
the process of selecting a jury when Hawkins busted out of the Criminal Courts
Building in the Los Angeles Civic Center
on November 27, 1985 and escaped. As it
turned out, the prosecutors couldn't have
gotten a more opportune break themselves.

Hawkins managed to hide out and stay
on the run for several weeks, despite pleas
from his father and other family members
for him to peacefully surrender. When police finally caught up with him in February
1986, he had travelled more than 150 miles
upstate to Contra Costa County near San
Francisco, the same area where Marcia
spent much of her girlhood. Contra Costa
County Sheriff's officers were forced into
a Wild West type shootout before he was
captured.

When police and prosecutors had an opportunity to take a good look at the guns
taken from the fugitive, they figured there
was a good chance one of them was the
same pistol used in at least one of the slayings in the double murder. The inside of
the barrel of the .44-caliber pistol had
been deliberately scored with a file or
similar instrument in an apparent effort to
alter the pattern of grooves that can provide a good ballistics technician with iden-

tification that's as surefire unique and individual as fingerprints.

Nevertheless, if it was true that Hawkins was personally involved in the slayings of the two men, and the gun confiscated after the shootout was a murder weapon, it was a terrible blunder on his part not to have permanently gotten rid of it.

Despite the efforts to destroy the one-of-a-kind pattern of grooves, laboratory analysis successfully matched the weapon with bullets used in the shooting of Grant. Bullets found at Turner's house by police and evidence technicians investigating his slaying were also traced to the .44.

Utilizing that information, Marcia called on ballistics technicians and other experts in the field in order to show that the weapon seized after the shootout was the same gun used in the killings.

Although she broke into the business prosecuting murder cases, Marcia found the Hawkins trial especially demanding in just about every way possible. Jury selection alone, droned on for six months. After the panel was finally seated, the trial itself ate up another thirteen months.

The trial of the notorious, desperate defendant was conducted under extraordinarily tight security. He was separated in the courtroom from spectators, including some of his relatives, by bulletproof glass. Several extra bailiffs were also stationed in the courtroom.

Hawkins had broken away from his captors once before and authorities were determined not to provide any opportunities for him to do it again. They didn't want to find themselves faced with an explosively dangerous break for freedom from the courthouse, or another wild car chase and shootout like those that had occurred in Contra Costa County.

More than fifty witnesses were called by the prosecution to testify. The entire process was an exhausting, trying ordeal that sapped energy and demanded every bit of concentration the trial lawyers on both sides of the courtroom could muster.

Marcia was up to the demands. She did a magnificent job of marshaling the evidence dealing with ballistics and presenting it to the jury. The jury deliberated for four weeks, and three members were dumped from the panel and replaced with alternates for one reason or another, before a verdict was at last reported to Superior Court Judge Marsha N. Revel.

The forty-two-year-old ex-convict and one-time heroic figure, was found guilty of first-degree murder and robbery. Significantly, the jury also found special circumstances existed including multiple murders, were committed during a robbery, which made him eligible according to the California Criminal Code for the death penalty.

After the verdicts were reported, Judge Revel advised the jurors of the convicted killer's previous felony convictions. He had convictions on his record for bank robbery and for armed robbery, when he shot Thomas and became an overnight, and short-lived, hero of the media and of the public. The judge later recalled the trial in a conversation with a reporter as being the ugliest judicial proceeding she was ever involved in.

Marcia's brilliance was proven perhaps even more dramatically after the conviction, when she gave one of the prosecution's summations during the penalty phase of the trial. The jury was more compassionate than the prosecutor, and wound up recommending twin life sentences behind bars, instead of a one-way trip to the execution chamber in San Quentin Prison.

It was August 1987 when Hawkins was finally sentenced, more than three years after the slayings.

Giss was an excellent mentor, and the young A.D.A. was an attentive student. Under Giss's tutelage, she got even better at her job, honing her in-court skills and other talents as a top-flight prosecutor.

Giss eventually left the sordidness and pressures of prosecuting homicide cases and turned his considerable talents to battling auto insurance fraud.

Her already promising career moved into high gear after she teamed up with Giss and worked as a full partner with him to win a victory in the Hawkins trial. It was her introduction to the Big Leagues, and she became one of the mainstays in the District Attorney's Office Special Trials Unit.

In her new position, Marcia was assigned to prosecute defendants accused of some of the most brutal and shocking crimes in Los Angeles County. Almost daily she rubbed judicial shoulders with some of the most disgusting slime and lowlife the City of Angels had to offer.

One of the most notorious cases she prosecuted involved the brutal murder of a couple of college students, whose bodies were found in October 1985 dumped in a field in the Santa Monica Mountains. The victims were eighteen-year-old Michelle Ann Boyd, a freshman at UCLA, and twenty-year-old Brian Harris, who was enrolled at the Northridge campus of California State University.

Four young men from a tough South Central Los Angeles neighborhood were picked up a few days later and charged in the slayings. A deal was quickly worked out to give immunity to one of the men, twenty-one-year-old DeAndre Antwin Brown, if he would testify against two of his former companions.

A former private security guard at the Los Angeles International Airport, Brown stated at a preliminary hearing that the college students were kidnapped while a couple of his companions were stealing Harris's car.

Later that night they were shot to death after one of his former pals explained "he didn't want no witnesses," Brown testified.

Brown, who was under special police protection, also testified at the arraignment. According to the one-time security guard's story, the killers drove from their Los Angeles neighborhood to the suburb in order to steal a car they could use in a robbery.

Boyd was walking the young woman from her apartment when the three defendants loomed out of the shadows. They never carried through with the robbery that was reputedly planned.

When the three remaining defendants were brought before Superior Court Judge David N. Fitts in Santa Monica for the proceeding, Marcia disclosed that Brown had been threatened with harm for testifying. A deputy sheriff discovered the threat when he intercepted a jail note being passed between two of the defendants, she said.

The message in the note disclosed there

was a conspiracy to keep Brown and another defendant from testifying, she stated in a written declaration. The prosecutor added that the note contained a reference to calling off "contracts" if Brown declined to take the witness stand against his former chums. The implication in the note was clear, she said. Brown and the other defendant were being threatened with violence in order to block their testimony.

The prosecutor and the sheriff's deputy who intercepted the note, were unable to immediately determine which of the two defendants was passing it to the other. She asked that the judge order Brown's former companions to provide handwriting samples to authorities, so they could determine who it originated with.

Judge Fitts said he couldn't order them to comply, but he agreed to ask them to provide the samples. He made a point however, of noting that if they refused to provide the handwriting samples, the prosecution could pass that information on to a jury at the proper time.

Marcia ultimately won convictions, and the killers of the two college students were sentenced to prison.

In 1991, Marcia prosecuted one of her most scientifically demanding trials, and won the conviction of Christopher Johnson after basing much of her case on a single drop of blood. Blood, and the unique DNA genetic pattern it contained, was the key to her courtroom triumph.

In some ways, the challenge she faced in winning a conviction against Christopher Johnson was even more awesome than the early troubles in the Hawkins case before the prosecution obtained the gun following the shootout in Contra Costa County. This time, Marcia didn't have the body of a victim.

The best she could do was to make scientific use of a single spot of blood found under the rear passenger seat of the car that Johnson was driving when he was arrested. Marcia drew on evidence developed through DNA comparisons with blood samples from relatives of the victim to prove that the blood spot in the back seat had come from the missing man.

The experience and knowledge gained about the new so-called genetic fingerprinting techniques utilized by forensic scientists which she used in that proceeding were put to good use by Marcia and her colleagues a few years later in the O. J. Simpson trial.

One of Marcia's more challenging cases, which she prosecuted earlier in her career, pitted her for the first time against one of the leading luminaries of the Los Angeles criminal defense bar—Robert Shapiro. Shapiro was representing Theodore Pacheco, a murder defendant accused of barging into the home of his estranged wife, Yvonne, with a shotgun and firing a fatal blast into her friend, Lincoln Godwin.

The trial had curious similarities to the O. J. Simpson case, which would pit Marcia and Shapiro against each other a decade later.

There would be efforts by the defense in the Pacheco trial to paint the dead man as a sweetheart of the wife, just as there would be hints during the O. J. Simpson trial of a romantic link between Nicole and Ron Goldman.

Shapiro's efforts to get Pacheco's five-year-old daughter to tell a different story from her mother's, fell flat during a preliminary hearing. A short time later, Shapiro worked out a plea bargain for second-degree murder, and the case never went to trial.

She was an excellent prosecutor, who combined her rapidly expanding skills as a trial lawyer with sincere sympathy for the relatives and other survivors of the victims of the homicide cases she was assigned to. She never lost the strong sense of justice nurtured in her by her parents while she was growing up.

Chapter Seven

Celebrity Stalker:
The Rebecca Schaeffer Trial

Good trial lawyers know how to take advantage of the slightest error or lapse made by their legal adversaries.

Marcia's ability to boldly capitalize on an apparent procedural mistake by an attorney in Arizona, served her well after she was assigned to prosecute the suspect in the shocking celebrity stalking murder of Hollywood actress Rebecca Schaeffer.

When she learned that a busy Pima County Assistant Public Defender had filed paperwork in the wrong court seeking to block the immediate extradition of Robert John Bardo to California, she dispatched two Los Angeles detectives on a quick late night airplane flight to Tucson to pick him up.

Paperwork for Bardo's extradition had already been prepared by employees in the governors' offices in California and in Arizona, when a Pima County Assistant Public Defender disclosed that she was going to fight the extradition effort.

A petition in requesting a mental competence examination for Bardo was filed in-

correctly. The problem was compounded
because the defense attorney believed there
was more than a week to file a writ of ha-
beas corpus seeking permission for Bardo
to remain in Arizona until formal extradition proceedings were conducted.

The documents were filed in Pima
County Justice Court, and Magistrate Wal-
ter Webber denied both the request for the
mental examination, and the lawyer's petition for a time extension to file the writ.
He said the court did not have jurisdiction
over the extradition, and designated the
Superior Court as the proper place to file.

Under the impression that there was
more time, the assistant public defender
didn't hurry across the street to the Superior Court to file the papers.

Marcia was keeping her finger pressed
firmly on events in Tucson since learning
Bardo was in custody there, and when she
learned by telephone of the procedural
miscue, she moved quickly. Since there was
no legal impediment at that point to prevent returning the suspect to California,
she sent the detectives after him.

The late night mission was carried out
with professional precision, but it wasn't accomplished without some shaky moments.
The clerk's office in Tucson was open until
midnight, and the assistant public defender
could have gone there before it closed and

filed the necessary paperwork to temporarily block the extradition.

Marcia and the detectives were in a race against the clock.

The two lawmen were booked on an 8:30 P.M. commercial flight at the Los Angeles International Airport, and their nerves were jarred when four separate delays were announced. The aircraft sat on the tarmac for forty-five minutes before it was finally given clearance and lifted off the runway headed for Tucson 500 miles away.

They arrived in Tucson at 1 A.M., an hour after the clerk's office had closed, and were met by local police officers who drove them to the Pima County Jail where Bardo was being held on $1 million bail. They took custody of the handcuffed prisoner at 3:30 A.M., and two and a half hours later they were aboard another aircraft with him, taking off from the airport in Tucson for the flight back to Los Angeles International.

The public defender learned about the startling overnight development a couple of hours later, at 8:15 A.M. after arriving at work.

Marcia's quick-thinking move to return Bardo from Arizona to California worked perfectly, and it drew effusive public praise from her boss at that time, District Attorney Ira Reiner.

Reiner, who was retired from office after failing to win a re-election and was later spotlighted as a special NBC television news consultant analyzing the performances of Marcia and other major players in the O. J. Simpson trial, told news reporters his deputy's action was perfectly legal.

At a hurriedly called press conference, Reiner proudly defended the action. He said it was made possible by a "momentary lapse" on the part of the assistant public defender in Tucson. The hurry-up sprint to Arizona to bring the suspect back to Los Angeles had his personal blessing, he said.

"This is not a game. This is murder," he observed. Reiner added that the police officers were sent to Tucson with his approval.

The handsome, white-haired D.A. pointed out, as everyone already knew, that Bardo was already in California. "It's a done deed," he said.

Marcia defended her own ethics and professionalism in pouncing on the opportunity, and told reporters, "I didn't act until I was certain it was the legally proper thing and the right thing to do."

Her audaciously unorthodox maneuver trimmed long weeks, possibly months off what could have turned into a long-drawn-out and expensive struggle over the suspect's extradition focusing on his mental competency. A protracted extradition battle could have caused a long delay in his trial for first-degree murder.

The quick-thinking and fast-acting deputy district attorney had pulled off a slick *fait accompli*, although it would still be awhile before matters related to the maneuver would be settled in the Los Angeles courts once and for all.

Bardo's Los Angeles County Deputy Public Defender took his best shot at turning things around by arguing Bardo was denied due process when he was whisked from the Tucson jail and flown back to California.

Stephen E. Galindo asked that the case against his client be dismissed in Los Angeles and Bardo be returned to Pima County for a hearing because he was "snatched" from the jail in Tucson and allegedly extradited illegally. In a motion filed with Judge David M. Horwitz in Los Angeles Municipal Court, he declared: "The courts should not sanction or condone unlawful police practices."

Bardo, with what appeared to be at least a grubby day-long growth of whiskers on his face, the hair on his head shaved close to his scalp, and one of his hands wrapped in a bandage, listened and watched from a glass-enclosed area as the judge postponed his scheduled arraignment to give the defense lawyer time to collect affidavits supporting the dismissal motion.

Eventually an appeals court upheld the controversial action that whisking Bardo back to Los Angeles was legal. Nevertheless, the unorthodox tactic landed Marcia in the middle of a fierce legal firefight that flared briefly in the courts of two states.

The subsequent first-degree murder trial also pitted her in a head-to-head courtroom confrontation with Dr. Park Elliot Dietz, the man who was probably his profession's most widely known expert witness and most outstanding forensic psychiatrist. They were on opposite ends on questions involving the state of the sanity of the accused killer.

Dr. Dietz, whose offices were in nearby Newport Beach just south of the city, was head of a three-year U. S. Justice Department study focused on violence against public figures, and stated after Rebecca's shocking murder that average people as well as celebrities can also become the victims of obsessive love. But average people have a less than ten-percent risk of being harassed in that way. Celebrities have a one-hundred percent chance of being targeted by "many such harassers," he said.

Bardo was a nineteen-year-old unemployed former janitor from Tucson, who was infatuated with the talented actress who played the role of the kid sister in the popular television situation comedy, *My Sister*

Sam which was aired from 1986 to 1988 until about a year before the slaying.

Authorities ultimately learned the high school dropout who was once a straight "A" student, had been obsessed with the cute actress with schoolgirl charm for two years. He wrote letters to her through her talent agency; stored a prized collection of personally recorded video tapes of her television show at his home; and talked incessantly about her to family members and acquaintances in Arizona, California, New Jersey, and Tennessee.

Bardo ended his formal education after his sophomore year at Pueblo High School while he was being counseled for mental problems, and spent some time in a mental treatment center.

He was one of three boys and a girl who lived with their parents, a retired U. S. Air Force veteran and his wife, in a working class subdivision in south Tucson. Robert had a sinister reputation among neighbors for his wild behavior and abusive, threatening ways.

They told stories about him leaping out of windows or hanging from the eaves of the single-story house and swinging inside the windows; of falling to his knees and scratching at the side of the house; and of playing hide-and-seek with imaginary characters in the front yard. The strange, frightening teenager sometimes ran around in the yard and scrambled in-and-out of the windows wearing only his underwear. At other times he lowered his head and charged full-tilt into a cement wall in his back yard.

When he thought neighbors were being too noisy, he pulled out a .357 Magnum or threatened to use it in order to intimidate them into quieting down. The weekend before Rebecca was slain, neighbors said he stalked over to a nearby home where a family was celebrating the confirmation of a little girl, and threatened to come back with the weapon.

"If you don't shut up, I'm going to get my gun and blow you Mexicans away," one of the neighbors later quoted him as shouting.

He didn't return to the party, and the following Monday morning he boarded a Greyhound bus headed for Los Angeles. It was a trip he had taken several times before in vain attempts to meet with the beauty he idolized.

About a week earlier he had quit his job as a janitor at a Jack-in-the-Box restaurant a short distance from his home. He had worked the grill earlier, but asked to be relieved of that job because he couldn't take the pressure.

Bardo exhibited wide mood swings, and

after one of his outbursts he often became sullen and uncommunicative.

Rebecca wasn't the only celebrity he had been fascinated with, and he got into serious trouble over his runaway obsessions. He was so taken with Samantha Smith, the ten-year-old schoolgirl who became an international symbol for world peace when she wrote to Soviet leader Yuri Andropov and visited him in Moscow, that he hitchhiked to her hometown in Manchester, Maine.

Bardo had telephoned off and on to the girl for months, and she spoke with him at least once. His conversations were long and rambling, and Samantha's mother, Jane, finally asked him not to telephone anymore.

In 1985, the fifteen-year-old Arizona youth was picked up by authorities a few blocks from her home in the quiet little suburban town of 600 just outside the state capital, and held as a runaway. Samantha, then thirteen, was killed a few weeks later with her father in an airplane crash. But Samantha Smith wasn't the only celebrity the disturbed young man focused his attentions on before Rebecca. She was simply the most unfortunate.

In *My Sister Sam,* the rising young movie and television ingenue played opposite to co-star Pamela Dawber. The hilarious show began earning high ratings for CBS as soon as it debuted in 1986. The talented starlet also appeared on the ABC-TV soap opera, *One Life To Live*.

Rebecca had already appeared in big screen productions, as well, including the film Dyan Cannon directed *One Point of View*, and the comic, *Scenes From the Class Struggle in Beverly Hills*.

Only a few days before her slaying, she returned to her comfortable modest West Hollywood apartment, home from Italy where she was filmed in a TV-miniseries based on the true-life experience of a crippled man in a wheelchair who was pushed to a watery death in the ocean by terrorists who took over the Italian cruise ship, the *Achille Lauro*.

In June, her mother flew to Italy to visit her while she was there for the shoot, and they talked about Rebecca's plans for her career and the future. The wholesome beauty didn't consider acting the be-all, end-all of her life, and discussed dreams of someday having her own family and of interests in other subjects such as archeology. She was thrilled when she found an ancient coin near the Roman Coliseum.

The well-thought-out and rapidly up-and-coming career the twenty-one-year-old red-headed beauty had launched with such success was the kind that the woman who prosecuted her accused killer had one day dreamed of for herself.

At the time of the vivacious, dimpled, and brown-eyed actress's murder however, Marcia was firmly entrenched in the Special Trials Unit, keeping busy at the grim job of prosecuting accused killers. She was already one of the mainstay trial lawyers in the District Attorney's Office.

As a teenager, Rebecca was one of those lucky girls with a look of fresh-faced innocence and beauty that made boys stutter and forget their own names and made talent scouts for modeling agencies sit up and take notice.

The daughter of Benson and Danna Schaeffer, a child psychologist and a professional writer in Portland, Oregon, she attended Lincoln High School in the Northwest coast port city. She was a popular girl and good student, and people were always telling her how gorgeous she was.

By the time she was a fifteen-year-old sophomore, she was already doing some local modeling. A year later she had launched the beginning of a successful career and left home. She roomed with six other young female models in a two-bedroom apartment in a Manhattan highrise on West 62nd Street while she worked her way up in the business.

She was with an excellent agency and did a few local commercials, then landed a job as an extra in a TV movie. One of her earliest and most important achievements occurred when she became a covergirl for *Seventeen*. She was also pictured in other magazines aimed at the teen and young female market, and flew to Japan for a few modeling jobs.

She shared many of the same qualities with Marcia, that had left such a vivid impression on the Deputy D.A.'s former high school friends on Staten Island. Rebecca was intellectual, boldly adventurous, and unintimidated by the experience of living in the big city and seeking out new challenges and dealing with them on her own.

She kept busy with her modeling, acting classes, horseback riding, hiking, and dating, and completed her senior year of high school at the private Professional Children's School on West 60th Street. Rebecca never became involved in the wild party or drug scene. Like the former Marcia Kleks, once she set her sights on a goal, she pursued it wholeheartedly. She was too smart to foul up her life and opportunities with bad habits or the wrong kind of friends.

Instead, she carefully built up her modeling portfolio and honed her acting talents, focusing her life on achieving her dream of making it big as a movie star.

Her big break occurred when she returned home one day and found a note from her agent taped to her door. He wanted her to board a flight for California, and take a screen test for the role of Patti Russell on *My Sister Sam*. The agent couldn't call her because she was so broke her telephone service had been cut off. Like many young people seeking success in modeling, acting or other arts, she hadn't vaulted to instant access to fame and riches.

That all changed when she won the part. The first two weeks after Rebecca relocated to the West Coast, she roomed with her new co-star and with Pamela's husband, actor Mark Harmon. The couple helped her move her furniture when she settled into her new home, a nice, secure two-story stucco apartment building in the Fairfax District of Los Angeles near West Hollywood and Beverly Hills. It was considered to be a comfortable, middle-class neighborhood that was safely removed from the dangerous evils of street walkers, crack-dealers, and drive-by shooters who plagued so many other areas of greater Los Angeles.

She was living there by herself when Bardo rang her doorbell on July 18, 1989, in the middle of a beautiful Southern California summer morning. By a tragic accident of fate, the front entrance intercom wasn't working and the actress slipped on a short-short black bathrobe, padded to the glass security door, and opened it.

A curly-haired young man wearing a yel-

low polo shirt and carrying a shopping
bag and a big manila folder was standing
a few inches away. He had a pair of rubber
sandals on his feet. A large glossy publicity
photo of Rebecca was inside the folder,
and he had been showing it around the
neighborhood, asking people if they knew
her and where she lived.

She recognized the man with the bag
and folder as a stranger she had already
chatted with earlier that morning about a
post card she sent him after he mailed a
fan letter to her.

The initial encounter was brief but pleasant. As he prepared to leave she smiled,
shook his hand, and told him, "Please take
care."

When he showed up again at about 10:15
A.M., she was apparently less tolerant of the
interruption and told him to hurry with his
business because she didn't have much time.

"I thought that was a very callous thing
to say to a fan," Bardo later recalled.

Without uttering a word, the slightly
scruffy appearing youth pulled a high-
powered pistol from the shopping bag and
shot her, point blank in the chest.

Neighbors heard the crack of the explosion as the single shot was fired, and they
heard the actress scream twice. "Why?
Why?" The agonized shrieks were horribly
blood-curdling.

The young man in the yellow shirt was jogging awkwardly away through an alley, fighting to keep the flip-flops on his feet, when Kenneth Newell ran outside and saw the actress lying on her back in the building entrance. The retired fifty-nine-year-old English teacher was sitting in his living room next door to her apartment building when he heard the gunshot and screams. The screams weren't the kind of screams someone makes when they're surprised, he later recalled. They were the screams of a woman who was badly hurt.

Newell hurried back inside his house to dial 911, then he hurried next door with a bunch of towels to try to stop the bleeding. But when he leaned over her, she looked like she was dead. Her eyes were already glazed over.

Rebecca was declared dead a half-hour later at Cedars-Sinai Medical Center after being rushed to the hospital by ambulance. Her parents in Portland had lost their brilliant and beautiful only child. And Bradley Silberling had lost his girlfriend. He was heartbroken.

During funeral services that were conducted in English and Hebrew for the actress in the small chapel at the Ahaval Sholom Cemetery in Portland, the slender, bespectacled Los Angeles man broke down in tears while eulogizing his slain sweetheart. "I met the most sparkling soul who I wanted to spend my life with. And her name is Rebecca," he choked.

Struggling to continue, he added: "She always said, 'I love to be held so close.' So please hold her close in your hearts because . . ." He was unable to continue.

As soon as her friends and associates in the acting business heard of the tragedy, they began speculating that the killer was a crazed fan who was obsessed with her. Rebecca was so outgoing and friendly, that no one could imagine that she had a single enemy. Police investigators had the same idea about the probable description of the killer.

A woman caller from Tennessee added fuel to the suspicions and supplied the name of a suspect when she telephoned Los Angeles homicide investigators and provided information that linked Bardo to the slain actress.

The tipster reportedly disclosed that he was obsessed with Rebecca, had written an affectionate and rambling love letter to her, and also threatened to harm her. He had telephoned the woman in Tennessee early the morning of the shooting and revealed he was near the actress's apartment.

Rebecca's father later told a local newspaper reporter that Bardo first wrote to her in 1986, and he appeared to be one more strange kid who wanted someone to pay attention to him.

The suspicions about the youth's possible involvement in the attack were proven right the next morning, after the switchboard at the police headquarters in Tucson began lighting up with calls that a man was acting crazy and fouling up traffic on one of Pima County's busiest freeways. Tucson Police Chief Peter Ronstadt and another of his officers heard the report on their scanner and personally drove to the scene. The police chief is the brother of pop singer Linda Ronstadt.

Bardo was dashing in and out of traffic, dodging between fast-moving cars and trucks hurtling like juggernauts along the busy freeway, when Chief Ronstadt and the other officer ran him down and took him into custody. He had climbed off a Greyhound bus that returned him from Los Angeles a few minutes earlier, and wandered onto the highway near the main downtown exit.

A Tucson television reporter, James Weider, who drove to the scene with a cameraman after they heard about the freeway fracas, watched as the youth was arrested by Chief Ronstadt and hustled into a police car. Weider thought he looked "looney," or "at best dishevelled and at worst drunk or stoned," according to his later courtroom testimony.

A police officer described Bardo as disoriented and said he was "playing tag" with cars in an apparent suicide attempt. He was driven to the jail, where he told police he made statements implicating himself in the shooting of the actress in Los Angeles.

Tucson officers faxed a copy of Bardo's mugshot to detectives investigating Rebecca's murder, along with other information they had gathered on the case. The Los Angeles detectives showed copies of the picture around Fairfax. People who lived and worked there, said the photograph was of the same brown-haired man they had seen roaming the area shortly before the shooting.

Bardo was arraigned on murder charges a few hours after being picked up on the freeway. The arraignment was conducted with the help of closed-circuit television, which permitted the defendant to remain in his cell at the jail where he was being held under suicide watch. He did not enter a plea or make any statements during the short proceeding. A few hours later he was on his way back to Los Angeles with the two detectives.

In addition to eyewitnesses whom Bardo had questioned about the possibility of their knowing the actress and where she lived, or who had seen him jogging from the murder scene, Marcia and the police detectives who investigated the shooting gathered a treasure trove of evidence to use in his prosecution.

Some of the most significant items of evidence were a .357 Magnum, a bloody shirt, and a paperback copy of author J. D. Salinger's popular novel about an alienated depressed young man, *Catcher in the Rye*. Detectives said the items were found near the murder scene after Bardo directed them to their location. The bloody shirt had been tossed on top of a building.

The prosecution was also prepared to show that Bardo had written a letter to his sister in Knoxville, Tennessee, raving about a woman he wanted and indicating that if he couldn't have her, no one else could.

Quoting from the letter, Marcia said it read in part: "I have an obsession with the unattainable and I have to eliminate (something) that I cannot attain." He didn't identify the actress by name in the particular phrase, however.

The Deputy D.A. announced that the prosecution would seek the death penalty in the case unless she could be convinced of a good reason not to. Then she cited documentation raising serious questions about his sanity as a reason that might lead her to settle for a life sentence.

A few days later, despite the unprovoked nature of the attack and the widespread shock the murder of the popular actress engendered in Los Angeles and around the country, the prosecutor revealed she would ask for the lesser penalty of life behind bars.

If he was convicted, it would be as a first-time offender, and she said she doubted that a jury would order the death penalty.

With the possibility of receiving the death penalty eliminated, Bardo agreed to a bench trial. Superior Court Judge Dino Fulgoni was assigned to the case and would hear the evidence and return a verdict without a jury. The jurist was himself a long-time veteran of the District Attorney's Office who put in more than twenty years as a prosecutor before moving up to the bench.

During the long months of preliminary hearings, motions and all the other preparation and activities that precede an actual trial, Marcia kept in close touch with Rebecca's heartbroken parents in Oregon. They flew from Portland to Los Angeles to personally meet with her, and like family members of other murder victims Marcia had sought justice for, they became strong admirers. She knew that the long, drawn-out pre-trial process could be diffi-

cult for family members to deal with, and
she worked hard to keep them informed
about what was going on.

Galindo had indicated he might use a
plea of not guilty by reason of insanity in
his client's defense. Bardo was taking
regular medication in his cell at the Men's
Central Jail, and Los Angeles Superior
Court Judge Jacqueline Connor had already ordered a psychiatric examination
for him.

Dr. Dietz videotaped his interview with
Bardo at the jail in September 1991, only
days before the trial was scheduled to begin. Rebecca had already been dead for
more than two years, and the man accused
of murdering her had observed his twen-
tieth and twenty-first birthdays behind
bars. Justice was moving forward with slow
but inexorable certainty.

With his face betraying the prison pallor
of convicts who have been locked up for
long periods of time, Bardo told the psychiatrist about his meetings with the actress; the pleasant seemingly harmless chat,
and the second violent confrontation that
led to her murder.

"I almost had a heart attack," he said of
his reaction the evening after the shooting
when he listened to a television report an-
nouncing Rebecca was dead. Bardo claimed
he had thought that he should "blow my

own head off and fall on her," immediately after the shooting, but instead he turned and fled.

He said he returned to the apartment the second time because he remembered a letter and a compact disc he forgot to give her.

Bardo also told Dr. Dietz about his fascination with other celebrities, as well as Rebecca, and of a trip to New York when he attempted to meet pop singer Debbie Gibson. While he was in the Big Apple he visited the Dakota.

One of his most disturbing disclosures, was the claim that he learned how to ferret out his victim's address through an article he read in *People* magazine about another celebrity stalker, Arthur Jackson.

The Scottish drifter, who had a history of mental problems, entered the United States illegally in order to stalk actress Theresa Saldana. He caught up with her a few weeks later, on March 15, 1982, outside her apartment and stabbed her in the chest ten times. He struck her with such force that he bent the long blade of the kitchen knife.

Theresa lived in an apparently quietly secure neighborhood in West Hollywood, a few minutes drive from the Fairfax District, when she was attacked. The slender, dark-haired victim who starred in the 1980 Martin Scorsese movie, *Raging Bull* with Robert

De Niro about prizefighter Jake LaMotta, was critically injured in the vicious attack, but eventually recovered and returned to acting.

Putting the information he learned from the article to use, Bardo said he said he paid a private detective agency in Tucson to obtain Rebecca's address. He showed investigators at the Anthony Agency a publicity photo of the actress and claimed he was an old friend who needed her address so he could send her a present. The agency passed the job on to another professional sleuth in Los Angeles who easily gathered the information by contacting the California Department of Motor Vehicles. The cost to Bardo was $250.

Months later California legislators changed the law and tightened regulations dealing with the release of DMV information to the public.

Bardo's defense attorney wound up declining to enter any plea at all for his client. It was a way to protest the way the accused killer was whisked back to Los Angeles from Arizona without an extradition hearing. So Judge Fulgoni entered a not guilty plea for the defendant.

Despite Galindo's refusal to base his client's defense on a formal plea of insanity, he indicated that his case would be constructed heavily on psychiatric testimony.

Bardo's mental state at the time he stalked the actress and then shot her would occupy center stage during the proceedings and be critical to the outcome.

The lawyer insisted that Bardo's obsession with Rebecca could be directly traced to his long history of mental illness.

When the case was finally ready to go to trial, Marcia was aware that one of the most critical tasks she faced was proving that Bardo knew what he was doing when he murdered the actress. Proving that could mean the difference between obtaining a conviction for first-degree murder and sending the killer to prison; or settling for his being confined to a mental hospital after managing to convince a judge or jury that he was suffering such diminished mental capacity he couldn't control his murderous actions.

Considering what was already known about the defendant's history of sinister off-the-wall behavior, it might have seemed that his defense attorney had most of the ammunition. Shooting the defenseless actress was a crazy thing to do. Bardo's actions when he was picked up darting between cars on the freeway in Tucson, and other strange goings-on simply added more fuel to the defense contention that he was not responsible for his actions because of mental illness.

Despite the defendant's reputation and history of obviously irrational behavior, the deputy district attorney had a lot going for her, however.

The insanity plea isn't resorted to by criminal defendants nearly as often as most people outside the legal justice system believe it to be. When it is used, it isn't very often and studies consistently show that the plea is seldom successful.

Jurors frequently show a tendency to be skeptical and suspicious of too much egghead testimony about such esoterics as rape trauma syndromes, dysthymic disorders, Multiphasic Personality Inventory Tests and Thematic Apperception Tests. They seem usually to be more comfortable dealing with factual matters and absolutes, rather than an admittedly imperfect science or profession that delves into deeply hidden psychoses and other mysterious esoterics of the human mind.

Did Bardo know what he was doing when he shot Rebecca, and was he aware that it was wrong? And how much control, if any, did he have over his actions?

On the eve of the trial, the Schaeffers received a long letter from Marcia handwritten on yellow notepad paper. She assured them of her personal interest and determination to win justice for their daughter. The proceeding was one of the first trials in the country covered by Court TV.

Marcia was fated a few years down the road to play a starring role in an even more spectacular and lengthier murder trial that would also be widely reported through courtroom TV and other elements of the news media and make her name a household word. She would become even better known than Rebecca Schaeffer.

As always, the Deputy D.A. had done her homework and was totally prepared when the Bardo trial opened. Weider was the first major defense witness, and described the behavior and the look on the defendant's face when he was being taken into custody as reminding him of the suicide victim in the blockbuster war movie, *Full Metal Jacket*. The television reporter said he watched as Bardo talked with the police officers, his head held down and his eyes peering upwards, and watched him again on a courtroom video screen.

"Robert was a very sick young man," he said he concluded.

During cross-examination by Marcia, the witness agreed that other factors besides mental illness could have been responsible for the defendant's appearance, including the fact that he hadn't had any sleep for forty-eight hours.

Sparks flew during the cross-examination

of Dr. Dietz. The respected psychiatrist stubbornly rejected Marcia's suggestion that the defendant was an attention seeker whose voluminous writings were filled with concerns that are common to teenagers rather than psychotic hallucinations.

Dr. Dietz diagnosed Bardo as a schizophrenic, and said the voluminous writings and symptoms of the defendant suggested mental illness.

"Taken as a whole, this is a sick young man. A normal person would not repetitively threaten to commit mass murders, kill the mayor, kill your teacher. . . ."

During closing arguments, Marcia acknowledged that Bardo was obsessed with the actress, but strongly contended that he was not insane. He shot Rebecca because he wanted to become famous as the assassin of a celebrity, she said.

"A normal person does not stalk and murder an actress," she conceded. "But this was less than extreme psychosis."

She repeated information from statements by Dr. Dietz that the Bardo family was riddled with mental illness, including his mentally ill mother who raised him along with a mentally ill brother and other siblings.

She also hit at Dr. Dietz, accusing him of passively accepting Bardo's story of how the murder occurred without challenging *its* truth.

In his closing arguments, Galindo described Rebecca as "a victim in the true sense of the word," a woman who did nothing to deserve her tragic fate. He said, however, that Bardo was also a victim, a person who was mentally ill and was neglected by his parents, the mental health establishment, and the courts.

Despite the testimony of the famous psychiatrist with the impressive credentials, Judge Fulgoni returned a verdict finding the defendant guilty of first-degree murder. He also ruled that Bardo was guilty of the special circumstance of lying in wait to kill the victim. The finding of special circumstance carried a mandatory sentence of life in prison without the possibility of parole.

Bardo silently rocked back and forth at the defense table, while the judge somberly announced his verdicts. As he was being led from the courtroom a few minutes later, Rebecca's distraught boyfriend strode up to him and called him a coward.

The slain actress's mother, who attended every day of the near five-week-long trial with her husband and was watching the proceeding with family members and friends, leaned over and left her own departing words with the convicted killer with the remarks: "You will have to live with your guilt for the rest of your life."

A few days before Christmas, the convicted killer appeared before Judge Fulgoni for sentencing. During a short but rambling statement, Bardo said he understood the magnitude of his act. "I do realize that what I did was irrevocably wrong," he declared. "If you believe it is just and right to send me to prison for life, then I believe it is just and right."

Minutes later, Judge Fulgoni formally sentenced him to life in prison without the possibility of parole. The judge recommended that he serve out his sentence at Vacaville, the California state institution for the criminally insane.

Several years later the judge reflected on the trial and Marcia's handling of the highly respected forensic psychiatrist who testified for the defense and contended Bardo hadn't planned to kill the actress, but fired the pistol in a moment of unpremeditated rage.

In remarks to the *Los Angeles Times*, Fulgoni recalled that the prosecutor had her plan of action all ready for the nationally known expert witness. It was obvious that whenever the psychiatrist tried to divert her, she not only knew what he was doing but had anticipated his efforts.

She was already waiting with a plan of

attack to counter his efforts. As usual, Marcia's habit of meticulous pre-trial preparation paid off handsomely.

Chapter Eight

Shotgun Murder in Church

Hard-pressed prosecutors aren't perfect people, and they've been known to get what they want from a witness, then forget about them while turning to the flood of new cases demanding their attention. The demands of the job and self survival for prosecutors tends to preclude taking more of a personal, long-time interest in witnesses.

There are too many things to do, and too little time. Becoming overly involved with some of the people prosecutors must briefly associate with during trials and preparation may also be destructive to their personal lives and careers.

But it wasn't Marcia's style to play hit and run with witnesses who cooperated with her when she needed to draw on their experiences, memories, and testimony at trials, then wound up needing her help in return. One such person was a frightened, desperate woman named Jeannette Hudson.

Worshippers at the Mount Olive Church of God in Christ in South Central Los Angeles were gathered together on a hot midsummer evening for a Friday night service and Bible class when a man barged in wearing a mask over his face and cradling a sawed-off .12-gauge shotgun.

As the church filled with screams, seventy-six-year-old Eddie Mae Lee panicked, scrambled to her feet and ran as fast as she could for the ladies' room. She was stopped when a blast from the shotgun crashed into her back, slamming her to the floor in a bloody heap.

The remaining members of the startled flock, cowered in their seats and against walls, moaning and waiting in fear while the masked gunman stalked down the rows of pews until he was a few feet away from Peter Luke.

There was another roar from the shotgun, and Luke was thrown back, his body shattered by the deadly shot from the weapon. The gunman appeared to be leaving the church moments later when he saw Luke's thirty-five-year-old wife, Patronella and fired a final blast into her body.

A few moments later, the gunman, along with a companion who was guarding the door, disappeared into the night.

The two women were killed, but Peter Luke survived the deadly and seemingly inexplicable assault. About thirty children were inside the church, but none of them were injured in the vicious assault.

South Central Los Angeles can be a dangerous place to live, and shootings, knife fights, and other forms of random violence were every-day and every-night occurrences. The young men Marcia prosecuted for the murder of the two college students were from the same rough-and-tumble South Central neighborhood.

But the bloody church invasion and shootings were indescribably outrageous, and shocked even people who were already hardened to the realities of street violence.

A massive police investigation was launched, and detectives rapidly began to focus their suspicions on two men, half-brothers Albert Lewis and Anthony Oliver. Lewis's estranged wife, Cynthia would normally have been at the church playing the organ on the night of the shootings. She missed the services that night, but her cousins, the Lukes, were there.

The old woman who was killed was a friend of Cynthia Lewis and her family.

Detectives learned that Albert Lewis had been stalking his wife ever since she left him, and that he sometimes had his half-brother, Oliver, with him. The investigators established a surveillance around Albert Lewis's house, and it paid off. He and Oliver were observed removing the barrel of a shotgun.

A search warrant was obtained and a team of detectives moved in. The remaining pieces of the shotgun and some shells similar to those used in the Mount Olive church shootings were confiscated as evidence.

The investigation began to take a nasty turn from there, however. Lewis had an alibi, and it appeared to be a good one. He advised police that when the church invasion occurred he was with his longtime girlfriend, Jeanette Hudson. She backed up his story, and police couldn't get her to budge.

Police and prosecutors realized that if they were to obtain convictions against Lewis, and his half-brother, they had to break the alibi. It was Marcia's job to deal with the girlfriend and to go over the alibi with a proverbial fine-tooth comb.

It wasn't easy to cut through the fear and distrust, and Marcia met with her repeatedly, going over details of the alibi and gradually gaining her confidence. The prosecutor eventually became her confident, and the hard work and time spent paid off handsomely.

Ms. Hudson admitted the alibi was phony. She wasn't with her boyfriend when the church shootings occurred. The woman disclosed in fact, that she saw the half-brothers with guns shortly after the murders— on the same July night in 1989.

Marcia took the information to trial, and backed up by the critical eyewitness testimony about the guns and other matters

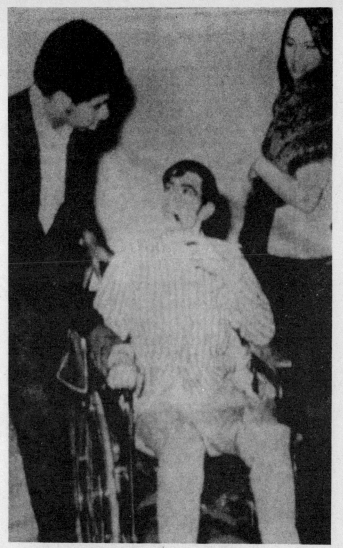

Marcia Rachel Kleks, 17, in her Susan Wagner
High School production of *The Man Who Came
to Dinner*.   (*Staten Island Advance*)

Deputy District Attorney Marcia Clark of the
Los Angeles Special Trials Unit with unit supervisor
David Conn. (*Andrew O'Brien/Sipa Press*)

Marcia with police investigators at the Simpson estate in Brentwood. (*AP/Wide World Photos*)

Marcia at a press conference just after Judge
Kathleen Kennedy-Powell ruled that there was
enough evidence to suspect Simpson of the
double murder.   (*AP/Wide World Photos*)

Marcia's drama training and intense dedication is revealed in this photo taken during the pre-trial hearings of the Simpson case. (*Sygma*)

A rare shot of Marcia in a lighter moment during the pre-trial hearings.　(*Sygma*)

Preferring to argue her case in court instead of the spotlight, Marcia limits her contact with the press. On October 28, 1994, she and William Hodgman toured the press room at the Criminal Courts Building to talk informally with reporters. (*AP/Wide World Photos*)

Marcia's meticulous preparation and forceful, articulate presentation make her the star of the Simpson trial.   (*Lisa Rose/Globe Photos, Inc.*)

Marcia concentrates on a particular issue during the trial proceedings. (*Globe Photos, Inc.*)

A team player, Marcia is well-respected by her prosecution team, William Hodgman and Christopher Darden. (*Sygma*)

Despite the pressures both in and out of court, Marcia keeps her sense of humor. (*Sygma*)

Marcia in one of her many confrontations with lead
Simpson defense counsel, Johnnie L. Cochran, Jr.
(*Sygma*)

Marcia confers with Cochran as F. Lee Bailey
looks on. O.J. Simpson remains aloof.
(*AP/Wide World Photos*)

Marcia Clark, one of the true heroines of our time.
(*AP/Wide World Photos*)

from Lewis's girlfriend, won the convictions. Interestingly, the 1993 trial was heard next door to Judge Lance Ito's courtroom where Marcia was to become such a prominent national figure a couple of years later.

The trial wasn't concluded, however, before more violence and fireworks erupted inside the courtroom. The half-brothers were mean characters, and when the thirty-six-year-old Lewis became upset over the testimony of one of the police detectives he doubled-up his fist and hit one of his own court-appointed attorneys.

The lawyer, Richard Leonard, punched his client back. Instantly, the courtroom was in an uproar. The two members of Lewis's defense team were brothers, and Jim Leonard joined in, while tables were knocked over and chairs were sent flying. Marcia managed to stay out of the fray, but Oliver was rushing to help out his half-brother when the detective witness joined bailiffs and other police officers to restore order.

Superior Court Judge Jacqueline A. Connor pressed an emergency button and summoned more help, while she ordered the alarmed jury panelists to get out of the room through a side door. One of the jurors fell and bumped her head before she was able to flee from the briefly fierce melee.

When the casualties were counted up,

Jim Leonard was found to have suffered a gash on his head. His neck and suit jacket were splattered with blood. His brother and co-counsel, Richard Leonard, had facial cuts and his suit jacket was split halfway up the back. Charles Lloyd, one of Oliver's attorneys, was hit by one of the tables but wasn't seriously hurt. He remarked later that during thirty years as a lawyer, he never witnessed anything like the courtroom fracas.

LAPD Detective Richard Aldahl, who was at the defense table to assist Marcia during the trial, was bitten on the wrist by Oliver. Judge Connor recessed the raucous proceeding for the remainder of the day.

Marcia later claimed in court that the defendants staged the brouhaha in an attempt to cause a mistrial. There was nothing about the testimony that could have been expected to set off such an outburst of violence, she pointed out.

Richard Leonard said, however, that his client was upset about evidence the prosecutor was expected to present about Lewis's ex-wife.

Lewis's ex-wife later testified she left him a few days before the shooting after learning he was legally married to another woman, and fled to Las Vegas where she was hiding out from him with her mother.

Neither of the obstreperous brothers was

in the courtroom when the jury brought in their twin verdicts against the co-defendants of guilty to first-degree murder. Oliver was in a hospital in critical condition, after another inmate at the Men's Central Jail stabbed him forty times.

Jail authorities reported that a twenty-one-year-old Latino inmate cut through the bars of his cell with a hacksaw blade, and hid behind a door until deputies appeared, escorting Oliver back to his cell in the high security unit following the court appearance. The young inmate reportedly leaped out and began stabbing Oliver with a shiv— a homemade jailhouse knife.

Oliver's half-brother, Lewis, missed witnessing the verdicts because he had tried twice to slash his own wrists and was on a suicide watch. He had already attempted to commit suicide two or three times earlier, since being locked up.

The courtroom was quiet and violence free when Marcia began her summation during the penalty phase of the proceeding. The presentation was typically strong and dramatic, while she argued passionately for the death penalty.

"These criminals violated the one safe haven we have in this troubled world, the place where we go to enrich and glorify what is best in us, where we reaffirm our faith in all that is good and righteous, where we renew our souls and seek solace in the spiritual from a troubled world, a house of God," she declared.

"This was no liquor store robbery. This was no bank-robbery murder. This was murder in a church."

The summation was devastating, bringing home all the out-of-control violence and horror that has become such a large part of contemporary American life. The jury listened entranced, while Marcia continued.

"We speak of justice for a defendant, but what about the victim? Is the victim to be forgotten? What about justice for the victim?" she asked.

"The notion of justice is not a one-sided thing. if we fail to make the punishment fit the crime, we have failed to do justice. And if the tragic deaths of Eddie Mae Lee and Patronella Luke mean anything, the punishment must be fitting. The death penalty may be the most you can do, but ladies and gentlemen, in this case it is the least that you can do."

Marcia pointed out that the two women were dead and could no longer speak for themselves, but she could speak for them and she was seeking justice in their behalf.

"I ask you ladies and gentlemen, for both of these defendants, Anthony Oliver and Albert Lewis, to impose the punishment of death."

The horror of the crime and the passion of the prosecutor's summation apparently convinced the jury that the dreadful penalty she demanded was justified. The panel returned a recommendation for the death penalty, and the half-brothers were sentenced to be executed.

One of Lewis's attorneys had speculated earlier in the proceedings that his client would not be given the death penalty because he wasn't the accused triggerman. Curiously, according to the prosecutor it was Lewis's half-brother who did the shootings while the outraged husband stood guard at the door.

Lewis and Oliver were transferred from the Men's Central Jail to death row at San Quentin Prison in May 1993, almost four full years after the shocking church shoot-out.

One more aspect of the case remained for Marcia to wrap up, however. Although it wasn't something she was required to do, the prosecutor repaid her debt to the witness who played such an important role in winning the twin convictions. She arranged for Ms. Hudson to obtain the help she needed to reassemble her life.

The Mount Olive Church shootings marked the last big case Marcia prosecuted for awhile. Soon after her hard-fought victory in the trial, she was moved into the job of special assistant to Hodgman in his new position as Director of the Bureau of Operations. It was a failed experiment, and soon after she moved into the slot and her marriage began to flounder, the forces were set in motion for Marcia to star in the biggest courtroom production of her life.

When she was assigned to early responsibilities in the Simpson investigation shortly after moving back to the Special Trials Division, her partner in the undertaking was her new boss and direct superior, Deputy District Attorney David Conn.

The Special Trials Division chief moved off the Simpson case after a few weeks however, in order to devote himself fulltime to preparation for the second trial of the Menendez brothers in the slaying of their parents. He was replaced on the Simpson case by Hodgman.

The two star prosecutors were ready to do courtroom combat with O. J. Simpson's highly vaunted, much-heralded "dream team."

Chapter Nine

The Simpson Murder Case

Everyone concerned, regardless of which side they were on, agreed on one thing when Los Angeles County District Attorney Gil Garcetti teamed up Marcia with her boss, William L. Hodgman, to head the case against O. J. Simpson:

They were legitimate LA D.A. Office superstars, who were fully capable of holding their own against the glittering squad of high-paid celebrity lawyers, consultants, and investigators that was still being put together to represent the defendant.

The "people" got themselves a top-notch team of highly skilled trial lawyers who had proven their ability to squeeze out victories in hard-fought cases.

Players in the heavy judicial drama had been working through the ponderously slow routine of pre-trial procedures for only a few weeks before O. J. trial watchers learned the startling news.

A shadow jury had secretly convened in Arizona and after a suitable period of deliberations, brought back "not guilty" verdicts for the man accused of slaughtering his wife and her friend.

When jury consultants and other experts helping to refine and shore up the prosecution's presentation of the case interviewed members of the panel they learned that a significant part involved Marcia's appearance and demeanor.

The jurors thought the woman in the severe gray or dark Navy blue business suits was too tough, ruthless, and bossy. They didn't like her. One of the shadow jurors was quoted in a report in a British newspaper as bluntly observing: "She's a bitch. You can tell."

It was the *National Enquirer,* however, that broke the story, reporting a focus group had determined the prosecutor was "cold and snobbish."

Some lawyers with a feminist bent were outraged at the revelation and made public statements attempting to paint the prosecutor either as a victim of male prejudices or as a turncoat. They ranted about double standards and equal rights, sexism, and behaving as if murder trials were tea parties.

But there was no indication Marcia had complained that she wasn't being treated the same as a man. No one was ferreted out and interviewed who could recall her ever behaving as if she labored under a special burden because she was a woman.

The prosecution had neither the time, nor the luxury of concerning themselves with political correctness, after learning the bad news from the shadow jury's deliberations.

The hard fact was, that as a woman who was achieving great success in a man's world, Marcia had a fine line to walk. She chose a profession for herself where, although some changes were occurring, she was surrounded by men. Most of the lawyers, judges, police officers, and criminals she worked with or dealt with were male.

In the unforgiving crucible of the courtroom, she had to fight hard and fight to win. Yet, she didn't dare to totally discard her femininity— or the special elegance of spirit and air of gossamer and lace that is generally associated with being female. Men, and many women, tend to be turned off by females who come across as too hard and aggressively masculine.

A real jury, presumably composed of the same kind of men and women, with the same prejudices, emotions, and likes and dislikes, would make the final decision on the defendant's guilt or innocence regarding two especially horrible murders.

And despite the high sounding pronouncements by judges and other court officers about avoiding emotional judgments about the appearance, demeanor, or personalities of prosecutors and defense lawyers in trials— people tend to be emotional creatures.

They don't simply discard old habits, ideas, and attitudes that have been ingrained for years, as easily as flicking off a radio or a television set for the duration of a trial. Jurors, like anyone else, don't have push-button emotions. If, for whatever reason, they don't like a defense attorney— or a prosecutor— there's a good chance their ill-feeling will color or help shape their decision.

It doesn't matter, when all is said and done, that it may not be the way court officers, lawmakers, and judicial scholars would prefer it to be. That's the way it is, and it's a cold, "immutable" fact of life.

If a real jury was convened and decided they didn't like Marcia because she didn't smile enough, had an unflattering hairdo, or was too sarcastic and bitingly aggressive during cross-examinations or in exchanges with opposing lawyers, the prosecution was in serious trouble.

Appearance is important in the courtroom, and not just for female attorneys. High-powered, egocentric, finely manicured male lawyers dress up in spiffy $1,000 suits; color, shampoo, style, blow-dry, and puff-up, or walk into court with carefully applied hairpieces. They're as perfectly dressed, coifed, and made up before going center stage as Tom Brokaw, Dan Rather, or Peter Jennings are before broadcasting the nightly news.

Even the defendants pay homage to the prejudices of appearance.

Serial killers and rapists like Richard Ramirez, the scruffy cocaine-crazed slasher and drifter whose ghastly depredations earned him a nickname as the "Night Stalker," showed up for his trial in a gleaming new suit and showing a reconstituted smirk representing hundreds of dollars in taxpayer money for repairs to his ravaged mouth.

Suspects dress to impress the jury, just as lawyers and other principals who play important roles in the courtroom do. Bikers and ex-convicts shave beards, cut their hair short, and cover up tattoos with long-sleeve shirts or sports jackets. Drive-by shooters and drug-gang hitmen, cut their hair and trade in their do-rags, sneakers, and blue jeans, for slacks, clean shirts, and dark shoes before appearing before juries.

Public defenders' offices in some cities maintain wardrobes of suits and dresses, shoes and accessories which they loan or give to poor clients who can't afford to buy their own. It doesn't matter that some of the men may never have worn a tailored suit and a crisply pressed, clean white shirt before; or that the women can't remember the last time they've stepped out in a lady-like dress, pantyhose, and heels. It's prescription dressing, and it's the way the game is played.

Soon after the distressing test run in Arizona, a new, more softly feminine Marcia began appearing at pre-trial proceedings. Journalists ceaselessly discussed in news stories and in columns the significance of calling in image experts to soften her flint-hard courtroom image.

The tone of her voice appeared to be a bit warmer, more pleasing and less harshly aggressive. And she smiled more often at Judge Ito, who had seemed to single her out for some of his most cutting remarks, leading to suspicion that he was put off by her toughness.

For the first time, almost four months after the slayings, she appeared on the steps of the courthouse for a bright, sunlit press conference. Her demeanor was as sunny as the weather, and some reporters thought she behaved almost giddy while she bubbled on about shopping, her boys, and her busy life.

Her laugh was more a charming giggle than a harsh smokers' cackle when in reply to a query she said, only half-jokingly, of the case: "It's ruined my life. We don't lead lives. What life?"

"She told the rapidly expanding crowd of reporters about the man who stopped her while she was grocery shopping in a supermarket and asked her to autograph a copy of the *National Enquirer* which had a front-page story about her. She said it was difficult to take her children to the park to play without being recognized.

What did she think about the mock jurors in Phoenix? "The media takes one kernal and blows it up into a huge bowl of popcorn," she said. It would seem from that statement, she was saying the decision of the shadow jurors wasn't such a big deal after all.

But it was difficult to deny that, Marcia had unveiled an extraordinarily different public persona than she had projected a few days earlier. The seemingly casual remarks about grocery shopping and taking her boys to the park to play projected a warm, motherly image that was radically different from that of a flinty-eyed, sharp-tongued prosecutor who was all grim seriousness.

The most obvious and dramatic evidence of the prosecution's effort at image adjustment however, was in the change she made in personal grooming and in her wardrobe. She had her hair cut stylishly short. She stored her power suits and sober pumps in a closet and went on a whirlwind shopping spree. Her wardrobe was expanded with five new suits and shoes.

The outfits she selected were made of softer fabrics and were lighter colored with feminine creams and pastels. One of the outfits was red with a dark collar and a row of gold buttons down the front. Another was cream with dainty piping. And yet a third, was an urbanely tasteful off-green silk. She wore a bit more tasteful and carefully chosen jewelry.

When she was seen on television, her image was studied, debated, and analyzed from head to toe. Journalists sought out the opinions of jury consultants and other experts in courtroom esoterics, and concluded that the prosecutor was being repackaged by Madison Avenue types.

It wasn't all repackaging, however. The reporters were merely seeing a side of the real Marcia Clark that her colleagues with the D.A.'s Office, the homicide investigators with the LAPD and the LA County Sheriff's Department, family members, and friends always knew about. She had a grand sense of humor, and could be warm and friendly; a fun person to be around.

It was the charming flip side of her personality that was part of the life she led outside the courtroom with her boys, with other family members and her friends.

And she seemed to truly love colorfully feminine clothes.

When the parents of the slain actress, Rebecca Schaeffer, flew to Los Angeles for their first meeting with Marcia, they found the prosecutor waiting for them, decked out in a charming pink outfit.

Marcia also got a new hairdo to replace the plain old utilitarian perm she previously wore. She took time off for a trip to a Studio City salon where one of her A.D.A. chums had her own hair done.

At the salon, her hair was trimmed closer to her face, so that it showed off her ears and cheeks. The shorter, fuzzier poodle-cut was set off with bangs, and framed her small face better, highlighting her best features so that she had a more relaxed and younger look.

Changes were made in the way her cosmetics were applied, to give her an appearance that was less flinty and more gentle. Crows feet that were beginning to crackle around her eyes, especially when she was tired, miraculously vanished.

Later in the trial after she tangled in a ferocious spat with the defense over a small angel pin on her lapel, Judge Ito barred her from continuing to wear it in court. Members of Nicole's family wore similar pins as a reminder of the dead woman. The judge had already issued an order banning anyone in the courtroom from displaying symbols of support for either side.

On the same day of the trial, as jurors were being recessed for lunch, he ordered them not to talk about the apparel or personalities of any of the courtroom personnel. He was no more specific than that, but some observers speculated that all the talk that was going on inside and outside the courtroom about the length of the lead prosecutor's skirts had a lot to do with the warning.

The dramatic makeover, especially her acquisition of a sparkling new wardrobe made good fodder for the tabloid press, daily newspapers, magazine columnists, and others concerned with such things.

But almost no one foresaw the serious repercussions it would have a few weeks down the line that would have a deeply personal affect on her domestic life and seriously threaten her responsibilities and privileges as a mother.

The media flap over Marcia's personal grooming and dress, was reminiscent of the talk that flared through the legal community and the press immediately after it was disclosed that she would would join with Hodgman to lead the prosecution.

Then, the private and public observations were of a more professional nature, focusing on her experience, abilities, and the way she handled herself in a court-room. The praise was almost universally effusive, and included plaudits from defense attorneys she had faced and beaten in earlier trials.

Garcetti said he selected the teammates because they had good chemistry between them, and the kind of background and winning track records needed for a big case like the O. J. trial. He said they would make up a formidable team.

Richard A. Leonard, a criminal defense lawyer who faced Marcia in a double-murder case, was quoted in the prestigious *Los Angeles Times*, as saying that any attorney facing her should know everything about his own case ahead of time. "She pulls no punches. She just plows straight in. And she's a formidable advocate," he said.

A law professor from the Loyola Law School, who was a former federal prosecutor, described Marcia in the press as "hard-charging." She also pointed out the need for Marcia to show her human side, along with her professionalism, if she expected to be able to establish a bond with the jury.

Chapter Ten

Enter the Dream Team

Preparation for the rapidly approaching trial was much more than sound bytes, fluff, and image however. Mostly, it was roll-up-your-sleeves, burn-the-midnight-oil hard work.

The prosecution team got together in an eighteenth-floor office set aside for the case, that was rapidly filled with a bulge of file cabinets, cardboard accordion files, stuffed manila folders and boxes of legal briefs and all the paperwork minutiae necessary to properly prepare for the approaching ordeal by fire.

The prosecutors and their back-up support team interviewed witnesses, went over fine and not-so-fine points of law, reviewed pertinent legal precedents in earlier cases, and joined in skull sessions with police investigators and with each other. Sometimes they rode the elevator, then trailed down the hallway from their own offices or from the courtroom to Garcetti's office, and traded tension-relieving quips or discussed matters of strategy with their boss.

Twelve-and-fourteen-hour workdays were

nothing unusual, and the pressure was increasing as the trial drew nearer. Love of her job and regular exercise helped keep her energy level high, despite the devastating hours she worked and the emotional drain.

Marcia was careful to make time in her busy schedule for regular workouts at a gym near her offices. Under the watchful eye of a trainer, she lifted weights, jogged, and grunted and groaned through calisthenics.

Both sides in the contest had put together impressively imposing teams of veteran trial lawyers, consultants, and researchers in preparation for what was expected to be a proceeding lasting months—but also would be the most publicized American criminal trial in history.

Some of the most sensational trials in America were held in Los Angeles during the past few years. Most recently, there was the Rodney King police beating trial; the first trial of the Menendez brothers, with a second scheduled to start soon; and the trial and conviction of Heidi Fleiss, the so-called "Hollywood Madam" for pandering, which was almost ignored by the media in the frenzy over the O. J. Simpson case. Earlier there were the trials of Charles Manson and loony homicidal members of his "Family" of drug-crazed hippies; and after that the gruelling two-year marathon ordeal over the Night Stalker killings and other outrages.

But the O. J. trial was bigger than all of them, and the defendant had the celebrity and the money to attract a formidable team of defense lawyers. Soon after the arrest, Robert Shapiro, a top-notch trial lawyer with a reputation as a tough negotiator who was especially facile at plea bargains, emerged as O. J.'s lead attorney. Shapiro operated from an office in Century City, and was also known for his insight into how the press can be used for his own benefit. He once wrote an article aimed at other lawyers that was appropriately titled, "Using The Media To Your Advantage."

Shapiro had been around the Los Angeles criminal defense scene for a long time, and defended various clients, including former porn movie queen, Linda Lovelace; television late-night talk show host Johnny Carson; baseball star Daryl Strawberry; and Erik Menendez.

In between his courtroom duties, Shapiro kept in shape at his Beverly Hills mansion, swimming with his wife in their pool, and punching a bag or boxing with sparring partners under the careful eye of a trainer.

Like many of his colleagues, he was one more example of the professionally incestuous relationship between prosecutors with the District Attorney's Office, and the glitterati of the local criminal defense bar. He had been a Los Angeles County Deputy District Attorney for three years before leaving for the big money opportunities on the other side in 1972.

Shapiro was joined on the O. J. team by F. Lee Bailey, who flew in from West Palm Beach. Bailey was a silver-tongued orator, who previously represented a motley array of defendants in notorious cases, including Albert DeSalvo, the man accused of being the notorious Boston Strangler; Patty Hearst after she was accused of joining in the criminal activities of her kidnappers with the radical Symbionese Liberation Army (he lost); won an acquittal for Army Captain Ernest Medina who was accused of contributing to the infamous My Lai massacre in Vietnam; and Dr. Samuel Sheppard, an Ohio osteopath, who was serving a long prison sentence for the murder of his wife. Bailey got him a new trial and won his freedom.

When Bailey got in trouble in San Francisco where a motorcycle cop stopped the lawyer's Mercedes and socked him with a drunk-driving charge, he hired Shapiro as his lawyer. Bailey was acquitted, but his California driver's license was suspended for six months because he had refused to take a sobriety test. Bailey was godfather to Shapiro's oldest son, and the two lawyers had a long-standing friendship that was about to be severely tested by the pressures of the trial.

The Florida-based lawyer had a reputation for treating witnesses during cross-examination as chunks of raw, red meat to be dissected piece by painful piece, then roasting and basting them under the heat of his ferocious mind and sarcastically glib tongue.

Gerald Uelmen, a mustached and bespectacled former mob-busting prosecutor with a hearing aid, was installed as another important member of the defense team. The fifty-three-year old expert legal tactician who observed his fifty-fourth birthday at the defense table, was retiring as dean of the Santa Clara University School of Law and had teamed up before with Shapiro in the defense of Christian Brando, who was charged with murdering the boyfriend of his half-sister. A ten-year prison sentence was ultimately negotiated by the lawyers in a plea-bargain arrangement for the famous actor's son.

From across the country in Cambridge, Massachusetts, a professor at Harvard Law School, Alan Dershowitz, was signed on as a consultant. Dershowitz was recognized as having special knowledge in the matter of appeals.

Barry Scheck, a forty-four-year-old New

York lawyer with special expertise on the legal and scientific intricacies of DNA fingerprinting was also recruited along with his partner, Peter Neufeld.

But the composition of the defense team and matter of the specific responsibilities of individual lawyers would undergo important transformations. Before long, Johnnie L. Cochran, Jr., joined the team, and the trial wasn't many days old before all the other defense lawyers took a back seat to him. In court, Cochran was known for his ability to relate to black jurors and win cases other lawyers may have lost.

The fifty-seven-year-old former prosecutor, turned celebrity defense attorney, was a longtime friend of the defendant. In the years before joining the Simpson team, he helped win an acquittal for Jim Brown, another football hero, of rape charges.

Most recently after actress Elizabeth Taylor asked him to help Michael Jackson, who was in trouble for reputedly sexually abusing a thirteen-year-old boy, he kept the case off the court dockets. Then he played a key role in working out a multimillion dollar out-of-court settlement for the singer with the youngsters family. The charges were dropped after the boy refused to cooperate with investigators.

In a courtroom tangle with Hodgman in 1989, Cochran won an acquittal for Todd

Bridges, star of the television comedy show, *Different Strokes*, who was charged with shooting a reputed drug dealer eight times during a confrontation inside a crack house. The victim of the shooting survived.

When reporters asked Cochran what he thought about Marcia as an opponent in the O. J. trial, he replied that she was "very focused." He added: "It's going to be a major, major, major matchup."

After Cochran took over as the lead defense attorney, Bailey would be called on for much of the cross-examination of prosecution witnesses, and Shapiro began to fade into a rapidly dwindling public role.

One more big player joined the prosecution team: Carl Douglas, another hip, streetwise black lawyer, who rapidly earned a reputation and sobriquet for himself as the "hitman" on the team, for his angry, pugnacious, in-your-face style of cross-examining witnesses or exchanging unpleasantries with opposing counsel.

From the beginning, Marcia took the point for the prosecution. Hodgman hovered at her side, providing a more bookish support. Although, like Marcia, he had prosecuted some of the nastiest murder trials in Los Angeles history, his best-known case was his successful prosecution of Charles Keating, Jr., for securities fraud. The story made headlines in the financial pages and on the front pages of newspapers around the country, and Hodgman was rewarded by his colleagues with the county and state by being selected as Prosecutor of the Year.

Judge Ito presided at the dramatic trial, and ordered the maximum ten-year prison term for the big-time convicted white-collar criminal. The Los Angeles Bar Association rewarded him for his solid performance in that proceeding and others by naming him Trial Judge of the Year.

The experienced prosecutor originally teamed with Marcia was the laid back, scholarly legal expert, who had the answers to knotty questions of precedents and procedure for the O. J. team. Hodgman had the ability to sort out complex matters of evidence and law, and present them to a jury in such a manner that they were easily understandable. He was the conventionally dressed, soberly stable pundit who provided the perfect back-up for his partner's out-front performance.

The prosecution was also beefed up with Deputy D.A. Cheri Lewis, a five-year veteran with the office who had tried eight murder cases and obtained convictions in all of them. She was given primary responsibility for researching the prosecution's pleadings.

Garcetti, who lived only four blocks from the defendant's home in Brentwood, was putting together a formidable lineup of heavy hitters of his own. And he wasn't finished.

Deputy D.A. Lisa Kahn was given chief responsibility for dealing with matters related to the admissibility of DNA as evidence in the trial. Ms. Kahn was known for successfully prosecuting the first DNA evidence trial in California history, winning the conviction of a serial rapist and robber.

But the most significant addition to the team was Christopher Darden, who moved into Hodgman's position after the D.A.'s Number Three Man succumbed to the incredible pressures early in the trial and was hospitalized. Although Darden's particular strengths and areas of expertise differed from Hodgman's, again the prosecution couldn't have made a better choice.

Just as Marcia had to balance the special social pressures of being a prosecutor who happened to be a woman, Darden had his own personal problems to deal with that had nothing to do with his character or ability. Like Cochran, he was black. And like it or not, that was important because race promised to be an undeniable factor in the trial of a black sports hero who was accused of savagely murdering two white people.

Unlike Cochran, who was on the other side of the courtroom, Darden was suddenly thrust into an up-front role prosecuting a murder defendant who was a black hero. O. J. Simpson was as popular among blacks as prizefighters Joe Louis and Muhammad Ali had been only a few decades earlier. And in racially charged Southern California, where the Rodney King police beating trials and the Los Angeles riots were still fresh on everyone's minds, the race of the defendant and of the new man brought in to help lead his prosecution were facts that couldn't be ignored.

If anyone with the Los Angeles County Prosecutor's Office could successfully balance the many complicated problems and sensitivities so implicit in the double murder trial, it was Marcia and Darden, who took on the responsibilities of co-counsel after Hodgman became ill.

The thirty-eight-year-old Deputy District Attorney came to the team with an impressive record, and he was a stand-up, tough prosecutor who was passionately devoted to his job. He had focused much of his recent efforts on policemen accused of misconduct. Suddenly, as an O. J. prosecutor however, he found himself being described in some neighborhoods and circles as an "Uncle Tom."

Darden, of course, had a lot going for him. He knew how to strip through the distracting glitter and glitz of testimony by instant celebrities, or the bewildering ambiguities of sophisticated scientific evidence, in order to get right down to the gizzard and guts of an issue.

All of his skills would be called on, because it would be his task to tear up the defendant's reputation as "Mr. Good Guy," an undertaking that would be ill advised for a white prosecutor facing a jury composed of so many blacks. By necessity, Darden would be the hatchet man.

The race factor had already been acknowledged when the trial was moved to the sprawling criminal justice complex downtown in order to draw from a jury pool that authorities said would be more "diverse." Because of the location of the murders in Brentwood, the trial normally would have been held at the courthouse in Santa Monica. But most of the people who live in that area are white, and there was concern about accusations of racism in jury selection if a mostly white jury was selected from that area.

Conveniently as well, the judge selected to preside over the case was neither white nor black. Judge Ito is Japanese-American and his parents met while they were in a California internment camp during World War II. The forty-four-year-old magistrate's wife is Margaret York, a captain and the highest-ranking woman in the Los Angeles Police Department.

As a judge, Ito was respected among his colleagues on the bench and the lawyers who appeared in his court for his ready intelligence, keen understanding of the law, and for being objective and fair. And it seemed that he was a good choice to deal with the special challenges of the proceeding.

Judge Ito took over as ringmaster of the proceeding soon after another judge, Kathleen Kennedy-Powell, concluded at the end of a six-day preliminary hearing in July that there was sufficient evidence to bind the defendant over for trial on twin charges of first-degree murder.

The bad blood between Marcia and Shapiro erupted on the first day of the hearing when they tangled over a mysterious white envelope she asked the judge for permission to open in view of the court and the millions of people in the television audience.

"It seems like a bit of grandstanding," Shapiro complained.

"Excuse me," the prosecutor responded, as if she wasn't sure she had heard him correctly. "I can't believe I heard Mr. Shapiro say that." The words "Mr. Shapiro" were emphasized. Marcia knew how to hold her own and to give as good or better as she got, no matter how imposing the reputation of an opposing lawyer might be. She couldn't be intimidated, and wouldn't back down.

The bitter exchange provided a good look at the kind of fireworks that were ahead. No one expected things to be pretty.

"The people have more than established their burden," Judge Kennedy-Powell nevertheless declared after Marcia finished presenting the State's case. "The defendant should be held to account."

Both sides in the contest also readied themselves with jury consultants. The defense hired Jo-Ellen Dimitrius, of Pasadena, as their expert. As the team's trial consultant, it was the forty-year-old expert's job to conduct surveys and carry out other tasks aimed at gathering clues to attitudes that might work against the defendant; to study prospective jurors and finally to advise the lawyers which ones she believed would be most favorable to her client.

Don Vinson was the jury consultant for the prosecution, and relied heavily on computer analysis of the responses of prospective panelists to an eighty-page questionnaire handed out to the candidates at the direction of Judge Ito. Vinson fed the data into machines at the offices of DecisionQuest, then passed on the results to Marcia and her colleagues.

Eventually, the prosecutors elected to go with their own educated intuition, fashioned from a mix of experience and gut feelings in order to select jurors they believed were most ideal for judging the case from their perspective.

During the jury selection process, candidates for the panel got a good look at the new Marcia. She was gentle, coaxing, and sympathetic. When the first candidate appeared to be a bit shaky, Marcia asked the woman if she was nervous. The woman conceded that she was. "Me, too," Marcia said.

It was an amazing exchange that might have been cause for some eye-rolling at the defense table where Marcia's brashly confident demeanor and tough-mindedness was well known, if such behavior hadn't already been banned by the judge. One of the defense lawyers later sarcastically remarked to the press, however, about the lead prosecutor's "personality transplant."

When the twelve-member jury was at last selected, there were eight women and four men on the panel.

Only one of the women was white, and she noted her father had been a wife-beater. One of the black women had worked with victims of domestic violence. Because of the nature of the defendant's history of abusing his wife, their presence was considered a victory for the prosecution.

The consensus, however, was that the defense wound up with the more favorable roll-of-the-dice. One of the male jurors was black, meaning that eight of the twelve shared the same race as the defendant. Another of the males, a fifty-two-year-old white-haired man who trained employees for Amtrak, reported he was a mix of Caucasian and American Indian.

A prosecution spokesman observed glumly that the State had to play with the cards it was dealt by the judge, and by the makeup of the jury pool. Polls showed the obvious, that blacks were more sympathetic than whites to the defendant.

Prosecutors had also tried for the best educated jury they could get, because of the plethora of sophisticated scientific evidence slated for consideration. But Judge Ito dumped several prospects because they regularly read newspapers and magazines, and he was concerned about the heavy media attention to the trial. Only two members of the panel that was finally seated, had attended college.

Fifteen alternates were chosen after a few additional days of the selection process. A majority of them were black.

Like the defense and prosecution teams, however, the makeup of the jury came closer to being formed in soft sandstone than hard granite. Changes in the composition began early, and dogged Judge Ito and other court officers throughout the trial.

Matters took a turn for the worse for the prosecution when Marcia got in trouble after it was publicly revealed she had asked the judge to get rid of the first contingent of about eighty prospective jurors. According to transcripts released by the judge dealing with a private hearing away from the jury pool and reporters, she suggested to Ito that many, perhaps most, of the prospects were lying because they wanted to get on the panel. She suggested that perhaps the jury candidates should be given polygraph examinations.

Jurors couldn't be expected to think kindly of a prosecutor who had described them as liars, if they learned of the remarks. And Marcia responded by saying release of the transcript was unfortunate. Her comments were taken out of context, and she was only joking about the polygraph, she explained.

Shapiro's response was brutal. He branded the comments as "one of the most idiotic statements ever made in a courtroom anywhere." By attempting to get rid of the

jury pool, prosecutors were shielding themselves "from their own stupidity," he said.

The fuss over the integrity of the prospective jurors and whether they were
auditioning or not was mean and cutting
and Marcia absorbed some hard hits. But
it wouldn't be the worst personal firestorm
she would have to endure before the trial
was over, merely one of the first.

Chapter Eleven

A Star Is Born

Opening statements which are presented by both sides at the beginning of a trial are designed to give a judge and jury an overview of the case, an early peek at what is to come.

But the O. J. Simpson case was no ordinary trial, Marcia Clark was no ordinary prosecutor, and members of the accused killer's "Dream Team" were no ordinary run-of-the-mill defense lawyers.

When the antagonists took the floor to outline their versions of the case, the presentations and the court's reaction were chock full of surprises. And before the testimony of witnesses was ready to begin, Marcia would play a major role in scrawling one more unconventional footnote in California judicial history and folklore.

Just before the prosecution opened its case, Judge Ito firmly rejected a defense request to permit their client to address the jurors and tell them he was innocent. The judge observed that there was no legal precedent for such an unorthodox move.

When the defense asked for permission

for their client to approach the jury and pull up his pantlegs to show scars on his knees from surgery for football injuries, Marcia vigorously objected.

"It's going to give him the ability to limp up to the jury box, get close to them and impress them with his physical presence," she complained. "It is only a blatant attempt to impress the jury with his charisma and star appeal."

The defense contended the scars were from old football injuries that would have so seriously hobbled him that he was physically incapable of so handily murdering two healthy adults.

This time the judge ruled with the defense, and agreed to permit O. J. to show off the scars from the injuries and the surgery on his knees.

In American criminal trials, the state has the first turn at bat, and Darden presented an hour-long statement focusing on motive. He began the state's presentation by stating the questions that were the keys to resolving the issues.

Thus, in carefully measured, unemotional tones, Darden patiently sketched a word picture of the prosecution's case for the jury. Acknowledging O. J.'s phenomenal celebrity, he cautioned the jury to remember the defendant wasn't there because he was a football hero or the likeable guy in car rental commercials. The defendant's carefully crafted public persona hid the man behind the image, who was a wife batterer, a stalker— and a murderer, Darden contended.

The Deputy D.A.'s tone was so measured and unemotional, at times that it bordered on boring. But he got the story told.

When it was Marcia's turn to address the jury, she introduced additional members of the prosecution team, then began expanding on the foundation her colleague had already laid.

The prosecutor was dressed in one of her new neat dark business suits, with dark pumps and a white blouse. Her make up artfully applied to emphasize her eyes.

"Why would Orenthal James Simpson, a man who seemingly had it all, commit such heinous crimes, throw it all away?" she asked.

"The one simple truth about the evidence described to you by Mr. Darden, is that it shows that Mr. Simpson is a man, not a stereotype, but flesh and blood, who can do both good and evil. Being wealthy, being famous, cannot change one simple truth. He's a person. And people have good sides and bad sides. Whether you see both sides or not, both sides are always there."

Referring to the Hertz car rental commercials the defendant was so famous for, she promised the panel would now see the other side of the face they hadn't seen before when watching the televised advertisements. It was a side that no one had wanted to see, she said.

"And that was the side that went from Rockingham, at his estate, to Nicole's home at 875 South Bundy on the night of June 12, 1994.

"Now, on that night, many events were happening at the same time. And in order to give you a true picture, a most clear and accurate picture of what really happened, how the events occurred," she said. "I'm going to go back and forth between the parties and between the locations."

She described the setting, the duplex condominium where Nicole lived with her two children, Justin and Sydney. The prosecutor pointed out that Nicole's apartment had a common wall with the apartment of her neighbors.

The defendant lived at 360 Rockingham Avenue in Brentwood, and Kato Kaelin lived behind the main building in a guest house. O. J.'s grown daughter from his first marriage, Arnelle, lived in a second guest unit that shared a common wall with Kato's.

Kato met Nicole at a party in Aspen, Colorado, after she split with O. J., the prosecutor explained. The young man and the woman continued a platonic friendship, and in 1993 Kato went to a party Nicole gave in Greta Green, also in Brentwood. He asked if he could rent a guest unit behind the house, and Nicole agreed.

Kato was prepared to go along when Nicole moved from Greta Green to the apartment on South Bundy in Brentwood, she said. Separate living quarters were also available for Kato at the new home, but although it had its own entrance and exit it was all under the same roof.

"The defendant asked Kato not to stay there, not to live under the same roof as Nicole, saying it wouldn't be appropriate," the prosecutor told the panel. O. J. invited Kato to resettle in one of the guest units at the estate on Rockingham, and agreed to allow him to stay there free.

"And so, in January of 1994, Kato moved to the guest unit behind the defendant's house on Rockingham and Nicole moved to 875 South Bundy."

Marcia showed the jury a diagram of O. J.'s home, pointing out the main house and the guest units, and explaining how locked doors prevented anyone from easily wandering back and forth.

"You see the area here?" she asked, pointing to the board. "It's marked 'Kaelin's room.' I don't know if you can all read it. That's why I'm pointing to it for you. That is Kato's guest unit."

After an interruption from the judge, who asked that she allow Cochran to step to her right so he could see what was going on, she continued explaining the layout of the estate. Then she said she wished to get into some key points that had to do with the timing of the events that occurred the night of the slayings.

"You're going to hear a lot of talking about that throughout this trial," she remarked. "I think I can guarantee that.

Marcia was honing in on the time-line, one of the most important elements of the prosecution's case. It was the crucial window, the seventy minutes she and her colleagues contended the defendant couldn't account for when he had an opportunity to commit the murders.

Continuing to stress the importance of timing to the case, Marcia said the prosecution would show that Kato last saw O. J., at 9:35 that night, at the latest. "He did not see the defendant again until after 11. In between those two times, at 10:15, a dog is heard barking, that the evidence will show was Nicole's dog, which fixes the time at which the murder occurred.

"At 10:45, Kato heard thumps on his wall and shortly after 11, he saw the defendant. An hour and ten minutes, during which the murders occurred, in which the defendant's whereabouts are unaccounted for," she declared, promising more later about that.

She noted that O. J. and Nicole's little girl, Sydney, had a dance recital scheduled at her school that evening. O. J. played golf and cards that morning, but planned to go to the recital at 5 P.M. to watch his daughter perform.

Referring to previous remarks by her colleague in his opening, she said Darden already described how O. J. behaved that evening. "He was in an ugly mood, morose, depressed, and clearly fixated on his ex-wife, Nicole Brown.

"He returned home after the recital and he spoke to Kato," she said. "It was approximately 6:30 to 7 P.M. Nicole was arriving at the Mezzaluna with her party. That was all of her family and Sydney and Justin."

Meanwhile, she said, O. J. was back at his home and had talked to Kato about the recital. "He (O. J.) wanted to tell him (Kato) about it, and he mentioned to him that Nicole was wearing a tight dress and he wondered how she'd look in that tight dress when she got to be older.

"During the course of that day, he also told Kato that he and Nicole were through. It's important to remember that the defendant would make statements sounding like he was cavalier about it, but the truth that we learned from the inside was that he was not at all cavalier about losing Nicole," the prosecutor declared.

"Now, while the defendant is talking to Kato on Rockingham, Nicole and her party arrived at the Mezzaluna for dinner, to celebrate Sydney's recital. Ron Goldman was a waiter at the Mezzaluna. He didn't wait on her table that night. But he was working there that night. Nicole was wearing a black halter dress and a black blazer. She left the restaurant with her family at approximately 8:30 P.M."

Between 8:30 and 9 P.M., O. J. went to Kato's room to ask for some change, she said. He was planning to take an 11:45 P.M. "red eye" flight from the airport that night to Chicago, and wanted change for the skycap because he had only $100 bills.

When O. J. said he was going out to eat, Kato invited himself to go along and a few minutes later they left the estate headed for a nearby McDonald's. O. J. drove them in his black Bentley. They picked up some hamburgers at the fast food restaurant, and O. J. ate his while he drove them back to the house. Kato kept his food for later.

"They got back to 360 Rockingham and the defendant parked his Bentley in the driveway, in the same position in which it was found by the police in the early morning hours of June 13th," she said. "When

Kato got out of the car it was 9:30 to 9:35, at the latest. And when he got out of the car, he last saw the defendant standing near the Bentley."

Marcia said Kato walked along the driveway, through the side yard back to his room, and made an immediate telephone call to a friend in San Diego. It was 9:37, the prosecutor pointed out. "So we know the defendant got home between 9:30 to 9:35 at the very latest. . . . When Kato left the defendant standing at the Bentley at 9:35, he did not see the defendant again until after 11 P.M.

"Now, what I'm about to describe to you is a series of events that proves that the murders occurred between 9:35 and 10:45 on the night of June the 12th, and that during that time the defendant's whereabouts are unaccounted for. At 9:37, Juditha Brown, that is Nicole's mother, called the Mezzaluna to see if they had found her prescription glasses that she thought she had left there at dinner that night.

"Karen Crawford, the bar manager at the Mezzaluna, took that call and went to look for the glasses. She found them out in the gutter near where the family had gotten out of their car to come into the restaurant. She brought them back to the restaurant, told Juditha that she had found them. Juditha asked her to keep the glasses there. So Ms. Crawford put them into an envelope marked 'Nicole Simpson prescription glasses.' " Marcia told the jury she would show photographs of the envelope to them later.

The prosecutor said Mrs. Brown telephoned Nicole at 9:40 P.M. and told her the glasses had been recovered and were at the restaurant. She paused in her recitation for a bare instant, but it was a break in her delivery that was pregnant with promise. "And that was the last time Juditha ever spoke to her daughter, Nicole," the prosecutor at last continued.

Marcia's theatrical training and years as a trial lawyer were paying off. She knew exactly when to pause in order to rivet the attention of a jury, and to squeeze out every bit of dramatic effect.

Resuming her story, she said a few minutes later Ms. Crawford received a call from Nicole and they talked. "Ms. Crawford then called Ron Goldman over to the phone. Ron Goldman spoke to Nicole for a few minutes and when he was done and he hung up, Ms. Crawford gave him the glasses and he took the envelope containing those glasses."

Shortly after that, at about 9:50 P.M., the prosecutor said, Goldman, still dressed in the white shirt, black pants, and black shoes he wore as his waiter's uniform, left the restaurant. His friends there never saw him alive again.

Marcia again turned to an exhibit, a graphic showing a view of the alley that separates the home of witness Pablo Fenjves from Nicole's condominium. The location where investigators later found Nicole's Jeep was also shown on the illustration.

"So at 10:15 a neighbor heard a dog bark. He remembered it clearly because the bark was like a plaintive, insistent wail. It was like nothing he'd ever heard before, although he'd heard dogs barking in the neighborhood often. Other dogs lived in that neighborhood; this was different. This bark sounded to him like a dog in trouble."

Continuing to focus on the time, she said when the neighbor went to bed at 11 P.M., the dog was still barking. "He went over to his bedroom shutters and opened them to look out in the direction that the barking seemed to be coming from. And he looked in the direction of Nicole's condominium, which is the direction it seemed to be coming from. And he noticed that there were lights on in the upper floor of her condo.

"When he fell asleep, shortly after 11, the dog was still barking. The evidence will show that this dog, wailing and barking so insistently, was Nicole's white Akita."

Continuing to trace the concern of neighbors over the agitated Akita, the prosecutor said Steve Schwab walked out of his house to take his own dog for a walk at about 10:30 that night. About five minutes later when he reached the corner of Dorothy and Bundy, which is perhaps one house down from Nicole's apartment building, he saw the Akita walking alone. The dog was agitated and appeared to be barking at the house on the corner.

When Schwab checked the dog's expensive collar, he noticed there was blood on the animals paws and legs. Although he didn't notice any injury on the animal at that time he figured there must have been a cut on the paw in order for there to be so much blood. As Schwab continued to walk, the Akita trailed after him, pausing to bark at every house they passed, according to the prosecutor's account.

When Schwab returned home at about 11:05, he and his wife talked about the troubled animal and what to do with it. They gave it some water because it appeared to be dehydrated, then decided to see if they could get it to lead them to the home of it's owner.

As they walked back the way Schwab had come and began to approach Bundy, the dog resisted. It didn't want to go with them, and pulled back. So they returned with it to the courtyard of their apartment building.

There was reasonably good light in the courtyard, and they could determine with more certainty that the Akita wasn't injured. But its paws and legs were definitely bloody.

Schwab finally wound up turning the dog over to a neighbor, Sukru Boztepe, to care for during the night. The dog continued to be agitated, however, and sniffed, scratched, and tried to get outside after Boztepe took him inside his apartment.

Consequently, Boztepe took the troubled animal for a walk, hoping it would lead him to the home of its owner. As it had when it was with Schwab, however, as soon as they began moving south on Bundy, the dog began pulling back. The Akita pulled harder and harder, until they reached the pathway leading up to the condominium apartments at 875 South Bundy. Then it stopped, and looked up the pathway.

Boztepe peered in the same direction, toward the apartments.

"And there he saw a sight that he'll never, never forget," Marcia told the rapt jury. "He saw the body of Nicole Brown lying at the foot of the steps in a pool of blood."

No one on the jury uttered a sound. The courtroom was silent, while the prosecutor again paused momentarily, allowing the grim reality of her words to take full effect. The grisly mind's eye picture of the bloodied corpse hung in the air as vividly as if it was projected on a television screen, and a good trial prosecutor knows better than to spoil a cogent moment like that.

At last, Marcia shattered the distressing vision and backtracked to events at the Simpson estate earlier in the evening.

"I last mentioned Kato at 9:37. He was on the phone to his friend in San Diego. He was on that phone for seven minutes," she said. "That call ended at 9:44, at which point, after trying to use the typewriter in that office I showed you before, which is right next to his guest unit . . . this must be the room right here— He called his friend, Rachel Ferrara."

The prosecutor hesitated, and Judge Ito asked her to finish her thought. She suggested it would be a good time to break for lunch. The jurist agreed, and recessed the trial after cautioning the jury not to discuss the case while they were away.

Chapter Twelve

Guilty As Charged

After the members of the panel filed back into the courtroom following the lunch break, Marcia briefly retraced her recent remarks to refresh their memories. She said that at about ten to 10:15 P.M., Kaelin was using the telephone again, while a limousine driver was on his way to the estate to take O. J. to the airport to catch the red eye flight to Chicago.

Although driver Allan Park's instructions were to arrive at Rockingham at 10:45 P.M., he hadn't been in the Brentwood area before, so he left early because he didn't want to be late, she noted. Consequently, the limousine arrived at Rockingham at 10:25 P.M.

"When Allan Park pulled up on Ashford street, he parked across the street from the defendant's residence, got out of his car, sat behind it on the curb and had a cigarette," she said. "He got back in his car about 10:30, sat in his car for a few minutes listening to the radio, and at 10:35 he decided he would go and look at the Rockingham gate to see if that drive . . . would be easier for him than the Ashford Street gate.

"Let me tell you right here, he was driving a stretch limousine and that has a very hard time making tight curves. He wanted to be able to pull up in front of the front door to an area that would be easy to load the bag in," she said.

"And so he wanted to see if the Rockingham entrance would be more easy for him than the Ashford Street address. So he decided to go down to Rockingham, drove the limousine down to Rockingham all the way down to the point where the driver's side of the window would be parallel with the Rockingham gate so that he could look inside.

"Now in doing that he had to pass right by the curb area, just north of the Rockingham gate. And what he noticed when he pulled through that area that was right in his field of view—that there was no car parked there. No white Ford Bronco. And it was 10:39. That's very important."

The prosecutor was methodical and unemotional as she continued. She was telling a story, reciting facts about the case as simply and straightforwardly as she could. The time for high drama would come later in her presentation, and after that when witnesses were called to testify.

She said Park peered down the driveway

and realized it would be more difficult to negotiate the turn there than "even Ashford." So he backed the limousine up Rockingham Avenue, turned left onto Ashford street, then pulled right up to the gate on Ashford.

"When I say he pulled right up to the Ashford gate," she noted, illustrating her explanation with a photograph of the area for the jury, "he actually had the grill of the car almost touching the gate, facing inward toward it."

Park looked at his watch after pulling up to the gate, observed that it was 10:40 P.M., and decided to press the buzzer on a call box that rings inside the house, she continued. When the buzzer rings, the occupants of the house can press a button and open the gate, the prosecutor further explained.

"At 10:40 he began to ring the buzzer. You could hear it sound but there was no answer. There were lights on upstairs— one light on upstairs. There were no lights on downstairs," she said.

"It seemed to him like no one was home, and he was a little worried about that, so he decided to page his boss and find out if perhaps the plans had changed," she said. "At 10:43 he paged his boss.

"He was then worried that perhaps the page didn't go through, so at 10:49 he called his boss at home, but there was no answer. He then got out and pushed the buzzer at the Ashford gate a few more times—still got no answer. Now during this period of time, Kato is still in his room on the phone with his girlfriend, Rachel."

Using another photo to illustrate her remarks, Marcia described the dark, narrow walkway at the southern edge of the estate. It was lined with a chain-link fence, shrubbery, and littered with leaves. She stressed that it was very dark and there was an air conditioner box. Kato's room faced onto the south walkway, she said. "There is no entry or exit there. He can't go out that way. If he wants to exit his room, he has to exit through the doors that are right there," she said pointing to them on the picture. "They're like shuttered doors, like shutters, doorlike shutters—and he goes through those shuttered doors to the pool area, and that's how he exits.

"So, on that night he's on the phone with his girlfriend, Rachel."

Moving on after expanding on the description of the area, with the help of the picture, she said Kato was talking to his girlfriend at 10:45 P.M. when he suddenly heard three loud thumps. She illustrated the effect by banging her fist three times on the prosecution table.

"The thumps were so loud that a picture

on that wall actually moved," she said. "Kato was alarmed. He asked Rachel, 'Have we had an earthquake?' When she said she hadn't felt any, he became even more alarmed, and then he wondered if there might be a prowler, somebody trying to break in.

"He was worried about the sounds he had heard. He was worried about those thumping noises, and so he decided that even though he was afraid and it was late at night, and it was dark, he should go and see what the cause of the noises might be," the prosecutor continued.

"A few minutes later, he hung up with Rachel and went out of his room to go and look."

Marcia said he walked out of the shuttered doors, through the pool area and emerged onto the side lawn that borders Ashford Street. "When he came out to that side yard, he saw the limousine that was pulled up to the Ashford gate. But he figured that the defendant had already made contact with him (the driver) and was about to let him in anyway, and didn't pay any further attention because he was very distracted about what the cause of those noises might be." Marcia said Kaelin was carrying a small, dim flashlight.

"In the meantime, just before Kaelin came out onto the side yard, Allan Park was standing at the Ashford gate, ringing the buzzer, still getting no answer. Finally, he heard the car phone ringing inside his car, and it was 10:52— he had still received no answer to the buzzing at the Ashford gate. He got back into the car and spoke to his boss, telling his boss, 'I don't think anybody's home. What shall I do?' His boss told him to wait a little longer, and when he'd been speaking to his boss for three minutes, he saw Kato coming out the side yard with his little flashlight.

"Almost simultaneously to seeing Kato in the side yard, he saw a person, six-foot tall, 200 pounds, wearing all dark clothing, African-American, walk quickly up the driveway and into the front-door entrance.

"Immediately, as that person entered the house, the downstairs lights went on. Allan Park hung up the phone and walked over to the Ashford gate and buzzed again. This time, he got an answer, and the defendant said— a voice that Allan could recognize as the defendant's— the defendant said: 'Sorry, I overslept. I just got out of the shower. I'll be down in one minute.'"

She said that although Kaelin was still distracted by the possibility a prowler was lurking around, and Park couldn't see well enough in the darkness to recognize the identity of the person entering the house— it was the defendant.

She said Kaelin decided to walk around to the south side of the garage and proceed down the narrow walkway, but when he got to the corner of the garage with his little flashlight it was very dark, and he decided not to go ahead. He was scared.

"When he came back around, he realized that the limo driver was still outside the gate. So, even though the defendant had spoken to him and said he was coming down, he did not open the gate for him. Kato had to go and open the gate. He opened the gate and he let him pull in.

"As soon as Allan Park pulled the limousine into the driveway, Kato, who was still very worried about the sounds, started talking to him, telling him he'd heard the thumps on his wall.

"Kato was very nervous, but now, with Allan pulled into the driveway and inside the grounds, he felt a little safer. So Kato decided to go back to the area and try and check out the sounds and what had caused them. When he went back to the south side of the garage, he went through a first gate that, basically, you just lift and push against the wall— it's not a locking gate— went up as far as a second gate, but couldn't see anything. It was still dark, the flashlight was very dim, and he decided to come back. He was too afraid to go back there by himself.

"Kato came back out around the garage, and when he came out, he saw that the defendant had come out of the house by that time. The defendant was now wearing a light-blue denim shirt and light-blue denim jeans. As he came out, Kato also noticed that there was a small, dark bag placed where the Rolls-Royce— excuse me . . . Bentley was parked."

Marcia's small, momentary bobble over the make of the car was unusual. She seldom ever errored even ever-so-slightly in her presentations; never missing so much as a syllable. She resumed her recitation however, smoothly moving on with the story.

"Remember, I told you the defendant parked his Bentley this way, facing out towards Rockingham. He could see that there was a small, dark bag on the grass near that Bentley."

As Kaelin helped the driver load the bags into the limousine, he talked again about the mysterious thumps he heard and of his concern it may have been a prowler or an earthquake, she told the rapt jury.

"So, he asked the defendant for a better flashlight so he could go around to the back area and check out the source of those sounds again. He and the defendant then walked into the house very briefly, but then the defendant said, 'Oh, it's late. I've got to go,' and came back out.

"While they were loading the bags, Kato offered to go and get that small, dark bag on the grass and put it in the car for the defendant. Unlike any of the other bags, the defendant said, 'No, no, no. I'll go get it.' He went and got the bag, the defendant got the bag, and put it into the car," she said.

O. J. never gave his houseguest a more powerful flashlight. And even though Kaelin seemed to be very concerned about the thumps, O. J. appeared "relatively unconcerned," she said. "He got into the limousine and they left for the airport at approximately 11:15."

Backtracking momentarily, the prosecutor said just before O. J. left, he asked Kaelin to set the alarm. Kaelin said he didn't want to. He had never set it before and didn't know the code. He was uncomfortable with the responsibility.

"No, I really don't want to do that," she quoted him as telling O.J.

"The defendant then left. They took off, they left out the Rockingham gate at 11:15. Kato went back to his room to call back his girlfriend, Rachel Ferrara, as he promised to do," she said.

"On the way to the airport, the defendant repeatedly complained of being hot. Allan Park could see that he was sweating, and he rolled down the windows and turned on the air conditioner. The temperature that night was 63 degrees. During that drive to the airport, Allan could see that the defendant was moving around with his bags in the passenger compartment, although he couldn't see exactly what he was doing.

"They arrived at the airport at 11:30, and that small, dark bag that the defendant insisted on putting in the car himself was never seen again after the defendant left for Chicago.

"Now, during the time the defendant was driving to the airport, Kato was on the phone again with his girlfriend, Rachel. During that phone call, there was a call-waiting interruption. The call was interrupted by the defendant. The defendant told him, 'I need you to set the alarm. I forgot to set the alarm.' He had to give Kato the security code and tell him where to go and set the alarm.

"There was a keypad outside the front entrance to the front door. Now, in the six months that Kato had been living there, the defendant had never asked him to set the alarm before, and never had given him the security code before. This was the very first time that had ever happened.

"Now, at this point we know the following. Let me talk to you about the timing again. Kato last saw the defendant at 9:35, when he was standing by that black Bentley after they'd come back from McDonalds. Forty minutes later at 10:15, we hear Nicole's dog barking that loud, insistent bark, that went on and on.

"And it would be safe to assume that it was very shortly within that period of time that the murders occurred. When Allan Park drove over to Rockingham and saw that the defendant's Bronco was not there at the Rockingham gate, it was 10:39, and so we know that the defendant had not yet returned home. The drive between Rockingham and Bundy was timed. Taking a normal rate of speed between the hours of 9:30 and 10:30 at night, it took approximately six minutes.

"So, at 9:35, last sight of the defendant. Forty minutes later at 10:15, the dog is barking. Nicole's dog is barking. At 10:45, half an hour later, we hear the thumps on the wall. This leaves us between 9:35 and 10:45 for the defendant to drive from Rockingham to Bundy and back, a total of twelve minutes, which leaves him a full hour to commit the murders.

"Now, let's go back to Nicole's home at 875 South Bundy. Now I'm going to show you what Sukru Boztepe saw when Nicole's dog took him to 875 South Bundy."

Using a crime-scene photograph, Marcia showed the jury a view from the walkway. Nicole's body was lying at the end of the walk.

"She's wearing the black dress that she wore at the Mezzaluna that night," Marcia pointed out. "Officers Riske and Terrazas were the first officers to arrive at the scene. They got there at 12:13. That's 12:13 A.M., shortly after midnight. They immediately contacted Mr. Boztepe and his wife, who pointed to where they'd seen Nicole.

"What you see here is what Officers Riske and Terrazas saw when they arrived at the scene. You can see here, the paw prints of a dog.

"Officer Riske will describe to you what it was he saw when he got there," the prosecutor continued. "They were the same paw prints, no shoe prints, only dog prints up and down this walkway. In order not to disturb the blood or any of the evidence, Officers Riske and Terrazas walked up the side where you see the bushes next to the walkway."

The prosecutor's presentation was interrupted when she prepared to show crime-scene photographs with up-close views of the grossly mutilated bodies of the victims. Judge Ito cut projection of the ghastly photographs from the television feed to the rest of the world.

Inside the courtroom however, the graphic blowups loomed over the proceedings from the eighty-seven-inch video screen that was mounted on one of the walls. The affect on spectators of the horrific images suddenly flashed on the screen was devastating. It was especially agonizing for family members of the victims. But Marcia forged ahead.

"You see here, Ron Goldman as he was found by Officers Riske and Terrazas. Now, what you're not going to be able to see in these photographs, ladies and gentlemen, is the fact that Nicole Brown's throat was hideously slashed. And you'll be able to see, and the evidence will show, that her murder took very little time to accomplish," Marcia said.

The picture was terrible; the gruesome remains of a tall young man covered with blood and lying on his side in the bushes. The coiled and distorted form was near a fence. His white sneakers, dyed red with his own blood, were near the camera. The white dress shirt he had worn was also drenched in blood and bunched around his shoulders.

"The same goes for Ron Goldman," Marcia continued, while gasps of horror broke out, despite cautionary signs Judge Ito had posted throughout the courtroom.

The judge had tried to cover all the bases with the warning, but human emotions, especially agony at such distressfully graphic images of the last moments of horror and pain the victims suffered can't be simply shut off as easily as flicking a light switch. Some of the spectators seated with family members of the victims, pressed their hands to their mouths. They lowered their heads, or unconsciously rocked back-and-forth on the hard pewlike wooden benches.

Goldman's father, Frederick, leaned forward, moaning softly in agony, while he jammed a tissue under his glasses to soak up the tears swelling from his eyes. His wife Patti reached over to her husband and draped her right arm around him comfortingly, while they shared their pain and loss. Choked, barely muted sobs flickered throughout the courtroom.

But Marcia Clark had a job to do, disagreeable as it was, and she pressed on with the presentation.

The jury and spectators were given yet another jolt, when a second bloody picture of Nicole was flashed on the huge screen. Taken from above, it showed the slashed-up body of the mother of the defendant's two youngest children curled in a fetal position among all the blood.

Display of the two ghastly photos of Nicole on the monitor, marked the first time they were ever publicly shown.

At the defense table, surrounded by his phalanx of lawyers, O. J., wearing a gray suit and print necktie, lowered his head and averted his eyes from the gruesome images on the video screen.

The photographs Marcia produced during her presentation, that flashed on the television monitor, were hideous, and stomach churning. The defendant's mother, Eunice Simpson was also among the spectators. A companion reached over and shielded her eyes.

The prosecutor picked up another picture of the crime scene, and reminded the jurists they were warned ahead of time they would be asked to look at some photographs that were unpleasant. She apologized for the graphic nature of the exhibit.

"But this is the crime that we're here to examine," she observed. "Looking down the steps, what the officer is pointing to is a ski cap and the glove that I've just shown you in the photographs. You can see it now in relation to Nicole. At the top of the photograph, you can just see the boot of Ron Goldman, and you can see the envelope in between them. That is the scene as it was found by Officers Riske and Terrazas."

O. J. began to show more animation, when Marcia turned to the photographs showing other items of evidence collected by investigators. He scribbled on a yellow legal pad; whispered to his attorneys; inhaled deep breaths; and as the prosecutor showed the jury a picture of the ski mask and a bloody glove, he tilted his face upwards and rolled his eyes.

Judge Ito at last ordered a break in the emotionally draining proceedings. Members of the Goldman family turned to the Browns and several of them joined their hands together; sharing their strength as well as their misery and loss.

Copies of the photos were not made available to newspapers or to television outlets. The judge had previously decided to ban their publication.

When the proceedings resumed, Marcia showed other photographs to the jury, various views of the crime scene, and yet other disturbing images of bodies and blood.

Officer Riske notified his supervisor about the murders, and the higher ranking policeman arrived at 12:30 A.M. A crime scene was immediately set up, and yellow police tape stretched in front and behind the residence to prevent anyone who was unauthorized from wandering into the area and disturbing evidence.

"After the arrival of his supervisor, Officer Riske entered the condominium," she said. "Now, what I should tell you is that when he came to the scene, he found the body of Nicole. He could see the front door of the condo, and it was standing wide open. So she had just come outside when she was attacked. He went inside, thinking that there might be a suspect inside and looked all through the house.

"Not only did he not find the suspect, but he found no evidence of ransacking, no evidence of forced entry, no evidence of a struggle— nothing that would indicate this was related in any way to a burglary," the prosecutor pointed out.

"When he got upstairs in that condo, he found the two children, Justin and Sydney, asleep in their beds. They were taken quickly out of the condo, out through the rear, to avoid the hideous sight in front of their house."

Marcia showed another photo to the jury, depicting bloody shoe prints on the walkway.

"You can see one set of bloody shoe prints as they go down the walk way. Those bloody shoe prints, that one set of bloody shoe prints, continues all the way back towards the rear alley area where there's a driveway," she noted.

Methodically, step by step, she moved past the blood trail to other matters; to talk of the use of DNA, commonly referred to as genetic fingerprinting; to hair, fibers, and other forensic evidence that was so meticulously collected and analyzed as part of the investigation.

Among other points, she noted that inspection of a ski mask found at the feet of the slaughtered waiter, disclosed hair matching the defendant's and fibers similar to those in the carpeting on the floor of his Bronco. Hairs matching O. J.'s were also on the victim's bloody shirt, she said.

Marcia was drawing a damnably vivid picture of a horrendous crime, and appeared to be successfully linking the outrage to the defendant with strong evidential links.

The prosecutor continued tracing the investigation in exhausting detail. She delivered a devastating opening— that apparently took its toll on her as well as others caught up in the emotions of the moment.

Curiously, after managing so well to maintain her composure during the desperately trying experience of showing the hideous pictures of the bodies of the victims, the normally unflappable Deputy District Attorney suddenly became very emotional as she neared the end of her statement. Marcia seemed to be on the verge of sobbing, or breaking into tears.

Her emotions flared when she described the defendant as a wife beater who bullied and dominated Nicole, and the presentation turned more agonizing as if she shared a deeply personal sisterhood with the dead woman.

At one point, she said O. J. beat, humiliated, and controlled his wife, ". . . after he took her youth, her freedom, and her self respect, just as she tried to break free, Orenthal James Simpson took her very life in what amounted to his final and his ultimate act of control," Marcia declared.

"And in the final and terrible act, Ronald Goldman, an innocent bystander, was viciously and senselessly murdered."

Judge Ito admonished her three times, warning her about straying from a setting forth of facts into becoming an advocate.

Undaunted, Marcia closed her opening arguments with authority and power of conviction.

All in all, Marcia had delivered a coherent, dynamic opening. Coupled with her colleague's earlier recital of O. J.'s sordid history of spousal abuse, they had built an ugly picture of the defendant and of the crime he was accused of committing.

The defendant's high-powered team of defense attorneys had their work cut out for them.

Chapter Thirteen

Three Ring Circus

The defense was about to take its opportunity to outline its case, when Judge Ito shook up the proceedings by threatening to close off future television coverage.

The startling development was set off when a remote control camera in the courtroom inadvertently caught a glimpse of one of the alternate jurors as she leaned forward. Televising the images of the twelve-member panel, or of any of the alternates, was strictly forbidden and the judge was furious. He recessed the trial until noon the next day, to give him an opportunity to deal with the problem.

When Cochran began presenting the Friday statement, it wasn't long before fireworks developed. The chief defense attorney had reached about the middle of his opening when he disclosed some surprise witnesses, including two lawyers who had previously done work for the defendant.

The shocking revelation brought immediate cries of outrage from the prosecution who contended the state was being sand-bagged. California state law requires that both sides in a criminal trial share information in a timely manner.

The lead prosecutor charged that the defense was guilty of "trial by ambush." Marcia complained to the judge about the newly disclosed witnesses and about other information in Cochran's opening.

"Morally, it's a violation of the juror's right to the truth. They've been lied to, they've been deceived, they've gotten half-truths from counsel, they have deliberately shown them items taken out of context," she declared.

Judge Ito was also upset and sharply reprimanded the defense for failing to come forward earlier and disclose the names of the witnesses as required in the criminal case.

The witness with the most startling testimony to offer was Mary Anne Gerchas, the forty-one-year-old owner of a jewelry store. She reportedly claimed she was hoping to rent an apartment on South Bundy Drive and was walking along the street at about 10:45 the night of the slayings when she saw four men running near the murder scene. Two of the men were Hispanic and two were Caucasian, according to the assertion.

Marcia asked for a thirty-day delay in the proceedings so the prosecution would have an opportunity to study the new evidence.

Judge Ito responded by recessing the court for the weekend, so he could schedule a hearing to rule on the prosecution request and determine what sanctions to impose against the defense. Prosecutors would have the entire weekend to figure out how the defense should be penalized, but the judge cautioned that he was uneasy about any idea of banning the defense from calling any of the surprise witnesses.

"That could be reversible error," he pointed out in a reference to a possible Appeals Court order for a new trial if O. J. was convicted after the testimony was barred.

The entire development posed a delicate legal conundrum; how to reprimand the defense lawyers for violating the rules, while protecting the right of their client to a fair trial. Among other things, defense lawyers are expected to try their hardest not to do anything that would damage their client's case or make him more difficult to defend.

When court resumed Monday morning, Judge Ito announced his decision. The prosecution request for a thirty-day delay was rejected.

The harried jurist also turned judicial

thumbs down on Marcia's request for an opportunity to counter Cochran's remarks that blood found under Nicole's fingernails didn't match her own, Goodman's, or O. J.'s blood.

Marcia was an excellent technician who had done her homework with her usual thoroughness and was knowledgeable about such things as blood and other bodily fluids, and how they are affected by the environment or other conditions. She was also thoroughly familiar with the crime scene, and wasn't about to concede anything to the defense she didn't absolutely have to.

She claimed the former prosecutor quoted information out of context from a blood test report, and contended laboratory tests didn't rule out Nicole as the source of the blood. Marcia claimed it had degraded because of the position of the victim's hand. Nicole's hand was clutching her neck under the body where the blood was warm and extremely subject to rapid degradation.

Although Marcia passionately argued the point, she lost that particular clash, almost everything else she and her colleagues asked for to even the playing field after disclosure of the surprise witnesses, was granted.

Judge Ito gave the prosecution the go-ahead to show four minutes of outtakes from a recently produced exercise video, "O. J. Simpson: Minimum Maintenance Fitness for Men." The former Heisman Trophy winner is shown on the video playing basketball, performing back stretches, marching, and doing push-ups on a desk. The video scenes seemed to provide a strong argument against defense contention's their client was so physically hobbled by arthritis he wasn't capable of killing the two healthy people in the manner they were slain.

Outside the hearing of the jurors, the judge delivered a harsh rebuke to the entire defense team for purposely hiding the identity of witnesses in order to gain unfair tactical advantage during the trial. And he banned the defense from calling any of the controversial witnesses until the final hours of the trial.

Significantly, he also ruled that the prosecution would be allowed to add to their opening statements, in order to deal with the defense claims tied to the newly revealed witnesses. The order was unprecedented in California judicial proceedings, and possibly in the history of other state and federal courts, according to some legal scholars. A similar move was permitted in a California civil case, but had never occurred in a criminal trial in the state.

Marcia was given ten minutes to deliver

the extraordinary additional opening statement. She used six.

When Marcia stood up at the prosecution table and approached the jury to deliver the extraordinary addition to the opening statements, she focused first on the exercise videotape and on remarks Cochran made about O. J. suffering from severe arthritis.

She recalled that Cochran had said the arthritis became acute sometime after O. J. was swinging his golf club at about 10 P.M., on June 12.

Next, Marcia invested a large portion of the six-minute statement to painting a scathing description of Mary Anne Gerchas. She revealed the prosecution had a new witness of its own, and declared:

"And, you'll be hearing a lot more about Ms. Gerchas in this trial, but right now I'm just going to address a few points that the evidence will show that Mr. Cochran didn't tell you about.

"For example, she spoke to her friend, Sheila Carter, the day after the murders of Ronald and Nicole. She told her friend, Sheila Carter, that she was not even at Bundy on the night of the murders. Mary Anne Gerchas had planned to look at an apartment in Brentwood on the night of the murders on June the 12th. The next day she spoke to Sheila Carter and said she did not go to Brentwood on that night, and she was glad because there had been murders committed there the night before.

"But Ms. Carter is also going to tell you something else in addition to the fact that she will tell you that Ms. Gerchas did not go to Brentwood on the night of the murders.

"She's also going to tell you something very important about Ms. Gerchas's credibility. She will tell you about a statement which proves that Ms. Gerchas is one of these people who comes out of the woodwork in these high-profile cases so they can get involved."

Marcia said the would-be witness sent her friend out to buy every issue of the *National Enquirer,* the *Star,* and every other weekly supermarket tabloid with stories about the Simpson case. Minutes later she concluded with the cutting remark:

"The evidence will show that Mary Anne Gerchas is a known liar and a Simpson case groupie." The statement was Marcia, at her acerbic best.

Chapter Fourteen

The Truth
and
Nothing But. . . .

Marcia was a full-fledged international celebrity by the time court officers and spectators filed into the brown wood-panelled Courtroom 103 for the beginning of testimony.

In daily newspapers across the country, on the front pages of supermarket tabloids, and on television and radio newscasts and talk shows she was getting more ink and air time than perennial naughty girl, Madonna.

The *National Enquirer* was leading the pack and sold millions of copies of the tabloid, featuring a blown-up photo showing the prosecutor just before her break-up with Gaby, posing topless on the beach at St. Tropez

The overseas press was paying more attention to her than Princess Diana, the Duchess of York, or to the ongoing fusses over the European Common Market, and the subdued activities of the Royal Family of Japan.

Across the street from the grim, boxy court building with the early 1950s *Dragnet* look, members of the media rented a plot of land dubbed "Camp O. J." for $24,000 a month and set up trailers and other support equipment.

One day an aging Cadillac powdered with rust spots pulled to a stop near the front of the courthouse and a transvestite dressed and made up in a pathetic attempt to look like Marcia, wobbled out of the passenger seat on a pair of high heels. A couple of reporters dashed toward him before his deep voice and a closer look at his 4 o'clock shadow made them realize they had been conned. After awhile when the Marcia poseur realized no one was paying any attention anymore, he limped unsteadily back into the car, and it pulled away.

Reporters for tabloids, daily newspapers, and magazines hurriedly worked up stories analyzing everything from the body language, handwriting, and horoscopes of Marcia, O. J., and Shapiro, to the stress levels of the defendant's tape recorded voice in order to figure out if he was lying.

Marcia, other attorneys, even witnesses on both sides of the surprisingly small courtroom— there are only fifty-eight seats for spectators— were showered with flowers sent by admirers and well-wishers around the country.

And Marcia was so relentlessly pursued

by the press that she moved out of her home and quietly relocated herself and her boys in an unassuming single-story house in Glendale.

If O. J. was the star at the beginning of the media and judicial circus, Marcia was the player who emerged at the last moment and stole the spotlight from him. She was the one whose image was most often being fed from the television monitors and beamed around the world, while the defendant drummed his fingers and watched her from across the room.

Back on Staten Island, her former high-school friend and co-star in *The Man Who Came To Dinner,* Harold Boyd, was among the millions of Americans glued to their television sets watching the trial unfold. "I was thinking, 'What is it about this woman that makes a bell go off?'" he later recalled. It was a nagging feeling that he wasn't seeing the whole picture, and was missing something.

Then another former high school friend telephoned and asked if he had seen the story about Marcia Kleks in *The Staten Island Advance.* Everything fell together.

The tenacious prosecutor who strode so purposely into the courtroom with a brief-case dangling from one hand, a load of accordion files stuffed under one arm, and a tote bag showing signs of long and faithful service hung over the other shoulder, was his one-time classmate at Susan Wagner High.

Boyd wasn't surprised that Marcia had become a woman of accomplishment and fame. "We all thought she was going to be an actress," he said. "But Marcia was always the type of person who could have been anything she wanted to be. So this is not surprising."

Boyd conceded that he hadn't recognized her however. Her name was different, of course. But the physical changes were most striking; her long, wavy dark brown hair was cut short, and her nose was smaller. Once he knew who she was, there were definite features and mannerisms he recognized, including the beauty mark over her lip.

"There is a special cantor she has when she walks over to the bench for a side-bar conference," he noted. "You can see the confidence, and she was like that in high school. She exuded confidence."

Marcia's confidence was especially obvious in court one day when she demonstrated how rapaciously quick and devastatingly cutting her quips and barbs could be during sharp exchanges with Bailey. A year or so earlier a poll had reportedly shown that the Palm Beach County, Florida lawyer was the best-known lawyer in the country. If Marcia knew about that, she didn't allow the information— or the lawyer— to intimidate her.

She behaved as if she loved to take him on, and jumped down his throat every time he gave her an opening.

The fireworks erupted during three days of gruelling cross-examination of Detective Fuhrman, whom the defense had been trying without much success to depict as a racist and Nazi sympathizer before the largely black jury. The prosecutor fiercely defended her witness, who had been taking a beating in the press for weeks, and was now all set up for another going over by the defense lawyer.

Bailey was doing his best to perform the kind of effective questioning of witnesses he was so well known for, and offered the theory that the police officer had concealed an incriminating bloody glove in a plastic bag inside one of his socks before planting it at O. J.'s estate. Both the famous attorney and the policeman were former Marines, and Bailey observed that Marines tend to carry things in their socks.

At one point, Bailey used another leather glove which he had in a plastic bag, as a prop and the judge was examining it. Marcia vociferously objected to the goings-on.

"This is ridiculous," she sputtered. "He's manufactured evidence. He doesn't like the truth so he's manufactured his own." She added that the glove was the wrong size anyway.

"Small size," she observed sarcastically. "I guess it's Mr. Bailey's glove."

Judge Ito ultimately ruled the defense couldn't show off a glove in a bag unless it was closer to Extra Large in size.

They tangled another time when Marcia demanded to look at sections of some books Bailey brought to court with him in order to help with the cross-examination.

"Ms. Clark always leaps before judging the size of the chasm," he sniped. Bailey pointed out the books were legal reference works, which he snidely claimed were probably way over the head of the witness. The defense lawyer offered to allow Marcia to read them, however.

"I think I probably read books with far more advanced technology than what are here," she replied acidly. "These are very basic primers."

"Dr. Henry Lee will be glad to hear about the insult," Bailey shot back. He was referring to a highly respected criminologist from Connecticut who was considered to be a possible witness for the defense.

The antagonists butted heads yet another time after Bailey told the court the defense had located a Marine sergeant who would testify he heard Fuhrman use racial slurs. "I have spoken with him on the phone personally, Marine to Marine," the lawyer soberly advised.

Max Cordoba said during an interview with a reporter for *NBC Dateline* however, that he had never talked to Bailey. Marcia, of course, knew about that and she tossed the information in the big-time defense lawyer's face.

"This is the kind of nonsense that gives lawyers a bad name," she declared. "Mr. Bailey— you can see how agitated he is— has been caught in a lie."

Bailey's fabled reputation as a cross-examiner *par excellence* had already taken a pounding when after nearly three days of frequently fierce cross-examination, he was unable to shake Fuhrman's composure. His face turned red. He was in a rage and when he attempted to interrupt, the judge advised him to control himself.

"I feel like we're in *Alice in Wonderland*," Marcia acidly added. "We got Jabberwocky. 'No' means, 'I don't remember.' 'I don't know' means 'no.'"

Ito asked her what sort of sanction she believed should be assessed on the defense lawyer, and she went for broke.

"I think that Mr. Bailey should be cited for contempt and fined substantially," she shot back.

Bailey claimed he never said he talked with Cordoba specifically about the sergeant's potential testimony in the trial. But he insisted they talked briefly by telephone and the Marine later remembered the short conversation.

Regardless, the famous defense lawyer was hung out to dry. And Marcia accomplished the feat before television cameras, for all the world to see. Sympathizers who were repelled by what appeared to be an effort to unfairly turn the heat on Fuhrman and make him, instead of the millionaire athlete at the defense table, into the virtual defendant in the case, responded by sending the tall, rangy policeman scores of letters and scads of flowers. A Pennsylvania man wired a $70 arrangement to him, and asked that it be patriotically done up with red and white flowers and a blue bow. The florist selected flowers that were all white.

The day after Marcia's dust-up with Bailey, Judge Ito ordered the two combatants to tell each other they were sorry. "It would thrill me to death if counsel would apologize to each other for the rather high level of vitriol yesterday," he said while sternly peering down from the bench.

Marcia responded at first with verbal wriggles and squirms, and for a moment sounded as if she was about to begin the dispute all over again. But the judge fixed her with another stern stare and she finally complied.

"I do extend to Mr. Bailey my apology for . . ." she paused, as if she was forcing herself to squeeze the rest of it out, but at last finished the sentence, "the extreme nature of the exchange yesterday."

Bailey peered down toward his lap while she added remarks about the exchange being "bad for the profession."

When she finished, Bailey got to his feet and also apologized. As he did so however, he looked at the judge, not at the prosecutor. Marcia busied herself shuffling papers.

Despite all the feisty prosecutor's rapid quips and comebacks, ready confidence and panache, no one knew at that time just how sorely she was about to be tested.

The crisis was triggered several days into the trial while the testimony of Rosa Lopez, the live-in housekeeper for a family next door to the defendant's Rockingham estate, was being videotaped outside the presence of the jury. Ms. Lopez was an important defense witness and her testimony was being taken out of the regular order before the prosecution completed its case, so it would be available in the event she left the country for her home in El Salvador. The witness was put off by all the media attention and other pressures, and serious concern had been raised about the possibility of her doing that.

Speaking in her native Spanish before a

video camera and the empty jury box, with translation provided by a courtroom interpreter, the maid contended during two days of testimony that she saw O. J.'s parked white Bronco twice on the night of the slayings as she walked her employers' Golden Retriever. She said she first saw the vehicle at 8 P.M., and again two hours later shortly after 10 P.M., just before she retired for bed.

Both times the vehicle was parked at the same awkward angle, the position it was in hours later the next morning when it was observed by police, according to her testimony.

About 11 P.M., she heard a voice she recognized as that of the former football star, she added. The witness was nervous and she was caught in a lie once about plans to return to El Salvador, but nevertheless her testimony appeared to provide important back-up for the defendant's version of his movements on the night of the slayings.

The woman's story had the potential of helping make his alibi stand up, and Judge Ito considered continuing the session on into the early evening. The jury was hastily summoned to the courthouse from their hotel rooms when it seemed they would be permitted to personally hear and witness Ms. Lopez's testimony.

But it was late Friday afternoon near the

end of a long, exhausting day in court, and the jury had barely shown up before they were sent back to their hotel again. Unfortunately Marcia told the judge she needed to leave so she could pick up her children and would be unable to attend.

Marcia left to pick up the boys, and when she returned to court Monday morning, she found herself the victim of oblique remarks suggesting that she used her children as an excuse to buy more time to prepare for cross-examination of the Central American witness. Cochran hinted that was the real reason, and the suggestion enraged Marcia.

"I'm offended as a woman, as a single parent, as a prosecutor, and an officer of the court to hear an argument proposed by counsel like that of Mr. Cochran today," she angrily asserted.

"Some of us have child-care issues, and they are serious and they are paramount. Obviously, Mr. Cochran cannot understand that . . . and I'm deeply offended."

Darden stepped in to handle cross-examination of the witness, and ripped her to pieces. Under his blistering assault she admitted she didn't know the exact time she saw the Bronco, and was shown to have lied time after time while she was under oath.

He also took advantage of his opportunities to suggest before the jury that she may have been trying to help the defendant because she disliked Nicole. Ms. Lopez's friend worked as a maid for the Simpson household and had been slapped by Nicole.

Sympathizers of the rattled witness sent her scores of floral arrangements. Darden also received flowers from fans, including one arrangement that was so large it required two men to carry it in.

Marcia's situation as a single mother was rapidly becoming even more complicated, and a good deal more threatening. Her estranged husband filed documents asking for temporary primary custody of Travis and Trevor. Gordon Clark claimed in the papers that their prosecutor mom was "never home and never has any time to spend with them."

This was no courtroom flare-up with Robert Shapiro over the perceived fibs of potential jurors, or a debate over the tone of her voice or the length of her skirts. Acerbic exchanges with opposing counsel were the kind of things that occurred in hard-fought trials, and she could assuage concerns about her image by softening her voice or changing her wardrobe. She had always been able to handle the stresses and frustrations of a trial, and often turn problems into positives. That was part of her professional life, and in fact she seemed to thrive on it.

She was also able to handle difficulties with the media, like the mistaken report by a local Los Angeles television station early in the proceedings that she was videotaped at O. J.'s Rockingham estate at least seventeen minutes before the warrant was issued. The report, broadcast on the noon-time news by KCBS, made her and the District Attorney's Office look bad, as if they had seriously fouled up. But the matter was quickly cleared up. A reporter for KCBS apologized, and the station retracted the story. The questions about the legality of the search raised by the erroneous report were settled and buried.

But helplessly witnessing her little boys being dragged into what was sure to become a widely public and publicized fight over their future and her qualifications and behavior as their mother, was the kind of frightening development that struck at the very core of her being.

Like many other working mothers with a foot planted firmly in both worlds, Marcia had managed to balance her time and energies while protecting her emotions. But her emotions were about to be whipsawed and frayed, while she became the reluctant symbol of serious problems of marriage and parenthood that had developed in America's rapidly changing society with the death of the nuclear family.

She was snared in an ugly catch-22 that confronts so many other working women who have to make difficult choices between their children and their jobs.

News of the sinister new sidelight that had intruded and added to an already bizarre trial flashed and rumbled across the front pages and the consciousness of Americans across the country. Immediately, people began taking sides and firing off verbal potshots in print and on the airwaves.

Feminists, fathers' rights groups, childrens' rights organizations; editorial writers, commentators, and talk show hosts; psychologists, psychiatrists, and family counselors—all the "experts" rushed to crowd on stage and chime in, offering their views on the social and political significance of the tug of war between a father and mother over their children.

They talked about working parents and the torment of mothers in the job market who can't find or keep work because they don't have baby sitters. They railed about inequalities in pay, fair pay, job training, day care, female consciousness raising, and the so called glass ceiling that prevents women moving up in their professions.

Or they talked about family and domestic courts where the odds were stacked against working fathers and routinely awarded custody to mothers, whether or not they were the better parent. They talked about child support payments that fathers never seemed to come up with, or about payments that were too high and crushed the life out of fathers with little money or property to share.

Shared custody, child-care needs in the work place, baby sitters who didn't show up or couldn't be trusted, nannies and movie horror stories about killer *au pairs,* all the nagging, hurtful pieces of the equation were brought up, examined, and spit out in public.

In an interview with *Newsweek* magazine, Roberta Cooper Ramo, president-elect of the American Bar Association, criticized what she said was a double standard. Fathers were admired for working hard, and welfare mothers were expected to work, but professional women were being told not to, she claimed.

It was the topic on everyone's lips from offices and factories, to hair salons and taprooms. Along with the glut of information, Marcia's domestic troubles generated a plague of misinformation, rumor, and gossip. And Marcia, who was locked in the biggest case of her career, was hopelessly mired right in the middle of it.

The former privacy that both Marcia and her low key estranged husband valued so highly, and protected for their boys had been destroyed by the media feeding frenzy.

Marcia's boss, Garcetti, stepped forward with a powerful plea for the public to be more considerate. News articles about the private lives of his prosecutor were very hurtful, he pointed out in a statement. Marcia and other prosecutors were being placed in a horrible situation by the media's delving into their private lives, he asserted.

Although a large segment of the media didn't appear to be listening, and responded with a blizzard of stories, Marcia had thousands of sympathizers around the country. She was swamped by well-wishers with a renewed flood of hundreds of letters and a mountain of roses and floral pieces. They piled up, filling offices with a gorgeous splash of brilliant color and sweet aromas. Courthouse employees lugged the overflow away, distributing them around area hospitals and nursing homes so that others could enjoy them.

Chapter Fifteen

The Good Mother

Gordon Tolls Clark filed the documents seeking temporary primary custody in the same Superior Court building where Marcia filed her divorce papers nearly a year earlier. The structure was part of the same grim complex of buildings that included the Criminal Court where the trial was being held.

The embattled prosecutor absorbed another jolt, when her estranged husband filed new papers with the Family Law Department of the court the next day accusing her of lying to a judicial officer— Judge Ito.

The twin filings were the first of a flash flood of petitions, motions, and pleadings that piled up in a custody battle that rapidly developed into vicious, openly aired matrimonial disputes.

Gordon asserted in the later filing that Judge Ito was misled by Marcia when she said she couldn't stay for a night session that was being considered. She was quoted as declaring:

"I have informed the court that I cannot be present tonight because I do have to take care of my children and I don't have anyone who can do that for me. And I do not want proceedings to go before a jury when I can't be here."

According to the assertions by Gordon, who had custody of the boys on alternate weekends, Friday, February 24, was his customary night to take the boys. He was to pick them up at 6 P.M., and was expected to keep them at his home until Sunday.

But his wife unexpectedly telephoned him at work late that afternoon and told him not to pick up the children that evening, he declared.

"Instead, she said she wanted to drop them off at my place at around 7:30 P.M. She dropped them off at 8:45 P.M. I had no idea at that time why (she) did not want me to pick our kids up at my usual time."

Gordon said he heard a news broadcast later in the evening and "immediately realized" why his wife changed their previously existing arrangement. He was saddened by her behavior, and as a father, did not think it served as a good role model for the children, he said.

The husband added that he would have understood if she wanted to be with the children, but he was upset at the idea she would use him and the boys to serve her own objectives.

Travis and Trevor were not ill Friday,

and even if he hadn't been available that evening, the housekeeper would have cared for the boys, he disclosed in the papers. The woman lived in during the week, and didn't leave Friday nights until he picked up the children and drove her home, he added. Her home is about ten minutes away from the family residence.

He said his estranged wife, "Clearly does not have any child-care problems. Any such implication is not accurate, misrepresents the actual facts, and does a disservice to me and our children."

His version of what really happened on the evening Rosa Lopez's anticipated testimony was interrupted was startling and troubling. It also appeared to add strong support for Cochran's intimations that Marcia may have been trying to pull a fast one by deliberately delaying the rest of the El Salvadorean maid's testimony until after the weekend court break.

There was "absolutely no reason why the children shouldn't be with me instead of continually being with baby-sitters," Gordon said in one of the filings. He claimed Marcia consistently turned thumbs down on his requests that she spend more time with their boys.

Most nights, Marcia didn't arrive home until 10 P.M., and even when she was home, she was working, he contended. By contrast, he was usually home every night by 6:15.

"I was always there for our children and assumed at least equal responsibility for their care," he said of his relationship with the boys.

"While I commend (Marcia's) brilliance, her legal ability, and her tremendous competence as an attorney, I do not want our children to continue to suffer because she is never home and never has any time to spend with them."

Marcia replied through a statement released by one of her attorneys, Richard Bloom. Lawyers from two Los Angeles law firms were representing her in the domestic dust-up. The statement read:

"I am devoted to my two children, who are far and away more important to me than anything. I feel it is inappropriate of me to discuss details of my marital dissolution case or child custody issues in the media."

Bloom added to his client's comments by asking that the public and the press respect her privacy.

Another of her lawyers made a strong statement to the press, describing her flawless reputation and sterling professional performance. He said there was no truth to any contrary claims by her husband. The attorney added that his client was disappointed her private family affairs had been made public, and had no intention of trying the marital dispute in the press.

Although that was obviously the troubled prosecutor's wish, it wasn't one that would be respected by the press. The media simply could not afford to ignore the messy family wrangle. Marcia was big news, and like it or not, her domestic problems were a big story. That was especially true, when her personal problems boiled over and became a factor in the trial itself as it was reputed to have done when she got the Friday night off.

Gordon was showing himself to be a fighter, who was fully capable of holding his own in toe-to-toe combat with his wife. In the process of carrying on their deeply corrosive personal tug of war, however, all the former couple's dirty laundry was being hung out to dry. And the District Attorney's Office and the role of its prosecutor trying the O. J. Simpson case were caught up in the fallout.

Suzanne Childs, a slender, striking woman and former television reporter, who switched careers to become a prosecutor, was in charge of the District Attorney's Media Relations Department, and did her best to keep the media off the backs of her colleagues. She was helped out by a staff of seven, most of them law students and most of them female.

Media leaks were impossible to completely avoid however, even for such a seasoned professional with her unique experience in both the information business and the law. Snoops from the print and electronic media were everywhere, and tabloid reporters who were expert at digging out titillating tidbits about anyone or anything at all, were leading the pack.

Tabloid reporters didn't settle for bones and scraps of information tossed out at carefully crafted press conferences, or wait endlessly in courthouse press rooms for telephone calls that weren't likely to be made anyway. They went out and dug up the story-behind-the-story on their own.

There was some talk in the halls of the courthouse and in the media that the wily O. J. defense team might somehow have a hand in the goings-on, but it was speculation— apparently no more. There was nothing to back it up, although it's doubtful that anyone on the defense team was heartbroken over the nightmare diversions closing in on the lead prosecutor's attention.

Marcia's sticky fight with her husband over his petition for modification of custody and the public dispute that it was stirring up, had the District Attorney's Office reeling under the weight of the media attention that threatened to shatter concentration and the cohesiveness of the prosecution team.

Even a well-oiled machine can't operate at its precisionlike best if one part suddenly begins developing a corrosive streak of rust, or scratches and pits in its surface. Hodgman had already been forced to the sidelines by stress, and now Marcia was being emotionally battered on two fronts.

Some of the heaviest hitters on Garcetti's staff of more than 200 attorneys were up to their briefcases in an exceedingly difficult and demanding trial that was being observed by millions of people, and anything that threatened to sidetrack their attention from their primary purpose was threatening.

The District Attorney's Office had lost some big cases, going back to the *Twilight Zone* trial after actor Vic Morrow was decapitated and two Vietnamese children were killed when they were struck by a whirling helicopter blade during filming of the movie.

A defeat in the O. J. trial would be devastating, and could dangerously erode public confidence in the ability of the District Attorney and his staff to get the job done. The pressure was on everyone from Garcetti's office who was involved in the trial, not just the harried lead prosecutor.

When prosecutors or defense lawyers are involved in a difficult case like the O. J. trial, it demands virtually all their attention and a huge portion of their time.

They must develop tunnel vision so that they "think trial." That doesn't mean that they totally abandon family life, but it does mean that many things have to be put on the back burner for awhile. Highly emotional distractions like the increasingly venomous custody battle Marcia was involved in, are especially draining and dangerous.

Although Gordon was protective of the children, once the paperwork was filed, it became available to anyone in the press, or to other members of the public who cared enough about the information in the documents to inspect them at the courthouse or run off copies. .

When the marital battle first began heating up about the time Rosa Lopez was testifying, a court order dating from the previous July was still in effect, but it was limited in the amount of information it barred from being released. The order only restricted access by the public to information revealing the names, ages, addresses, and dates and places of birth of the boys, and the addresses, telephone numbers, and Social Security numbers of the parents.

Marcia and her lawyers wanted an order with more teeth in it. She wanted the files closed to the press and the public, and a muzzle put on lawyers to prevent them from talking to outsiders about the case.

On Friday, March 3, her attorneys filed a petition in Superior Court asking the court to seal the file on the case and issue a protective order.

Curiously, in light of all the publicity she was getting and of how often her name appeared in print, in the space on the documents for "petitioner/plaintiff," and on some other pages her name was misspelled as "Marsha." The misspelling appeared on documents here and there throughout the case.

More importantly, both Gordon and some elements of the media opposed the move to seal the records.

In a brief filed by Marcia's attorneys supporting the motion to seal the files, her attorneys contended that Gordon "begrudgingly acknowledges that a seal on the file and confidentiality order are appropriate remedies to protect private and financial information."

They claimed the estranged husband's primary concern however seemed to be that if the orders were approved they would restrict his " 'First Amendment right' to call his wife a liar in the media and to defend himself from radio and television commentators."

His right "to discuss his disputes over custody and support issues publicly is not more compelling than his minor children's privacy interest, and must yield to that interest," Marcia's attorneys contended in the petition however. They added that the quickest way to limit public discussion is to approve the request and cut the media off from access to the case.

"In Biblical times, King Solomon was asked to choose between the competing requests of two self-proclaimed parents," it was continued in the document. "There, one parent was willing to give up her own rights in favor of the child's obvious best interest. In this case, the Court finds itself in a Solomonic dilemma, where significant competing interests are at stake.

"Petitioner desires to protect her children, even if it means she must forego opportunities to 'defend' herself publicly as a parent, which she is otherwise most eager to do (particularly with respect to comments she made to Judge Ito)."

They went on in the petition to accuse Gordon of focusing on himself and showing more concern for his right "to involve the media as a not-so-silent third party in this marital dissolution proceeding. In so doing, Respondent (Gordon) totally ignores what serves the obvious best interest of his own two children."

Gordon was criticized for accusing Marcia of lying to Judge Ito in a "mean-spirited declaration . . . prepared, filed, and leaked to the press.

"The country, if not the world, was already hanging with baited breath on the *Simpson* case," the document continued. "What in the world did Respondent and his attorneys think would happen when they chose to slander Petitioner's (Marcia) integrity in that declaration?"

Marcia also declared in court documents placed on file on March 6, that her husband told her on at least ten different occasions during the past several months that he might give an interview to the *National Enquirer,* because the tabloid was offering him a large amount of money.

"He stated 'I want to go to the *National Enquirer'* as recently as our Conciliation Court session approximately two weeks ago," she said. She added that she believed he knew how deeply upsetting to her his statements about the possibility of agreeing to a tabloid interview were. She said she also believed he was preparing to do more than make his court pleadings available to the media.

In the brief supporting the petition to seal the files on the case, Gordon was described as "championing his so-called First Amendment right to publicly humiliate his children," and of ignoring the needs and welfare of the boys by his behavior.

There was no question Gordon had taken the gloves off and was playing hard ball. But the husband in the case was also taking heat from several sources, and his critics were organizing and circling. He was soon complaining that he was being unfairly depicted as a vengeful man by high-profile feminists and some elements of the media.

In new court documents he defended himself for opposing a confidentiality order, by declaring that he was unaware of any "dire behavior" either by Marcia or by himself that would harm or traumatize the children if the information became public knowledge. "Petitioner (Marcia) is alluding to inflammatory events which simply do not exist for the express purpose of alarming the Court into sealing the file and imposing a gag order," he declared. "It is exactly these sorts of allusions that prompt me to resist the requested orders."

The athletically built, mustached father noted that he was the subject of intense media scrutiny, as a result of the marital dispute. Consequently he was being barraged with shocking accusations and falsehoods, "and no one is stepping up to defend me." He insisted he was doing his best to stay out of the public eye, but desperately needed to protect his option of speaking out to defend his actions and character.

"A gag order will not prevent the media, women's rights advocates, and other parties with their own agendas and interests from speculating on the facts of this case, or even in vilifying me before the mass media," he asserted.

During the past two weeks, he said, he learned that (feminist lawyers) Gloria Allred and Leslie Abramson were on the *Which Way LA* radio show, where they "speculated that I was possibly some kind of child molester, and that my motivation might be just to 'hit' Petitioner (Marcia) with the custody motion in order to get out of my support obligation."

During an appearance on the *This Week with David Brinkley* show, television news personality Cokie Roberts "implied strongly, that my case was being run by O. J. Simpson's defense team," he added.

Gordon said numerous news stories and editorials in magazines and newspapers incorrectly claimed he was seeking "sole" custody of his children. He was asking joint custody, with primary physical custody, he stressed.

He concluded by denying he ever stated he "wanted to go to the *National Enquirer*," but agreed he told his estranged wife that representatives of the tabloid were after him and offered him "a lot of money."

Gordon also added that, in fact, he understood that Marcia had been in contact with various elements of the media, including the supermarket tabloid.

An interim order was ultimately issued sealing the divorce and custody files. Attorneys were also barred by the decree from talking about the case outside the court. It was an important victory for Marcia, but it wasn't time for any large-scale celebrations. The proceedings leading up to the order represented only a skirmish, and the victory could turn out to be one that was fleeting.

The order furthermore, didn't prevent reporters from doing their best to track down the information from other sources independent of the court and of the courthouse. Most significantly, the order wasn't permanent, merely a temporary stop-gap. Lawyers on both sides of the dispute would still have to return and argue out the matter again later.

Throughout the bitter dispute, as legal papers fluttered back and forth between the warring parties, names of the boys were appropriately blacked out wherever they were referred to. But shielding their identification was an exercise in futility.

Their names had already been ferreted out by the press.

Fueled by public curiosity over the tantalizing details of the custody struggle, zealous journalists dug out other information about the prosecutor's private life as well, that included a bit of everything from her childhood to her daily routine during the trial.

According to the enterprising snoops, she was up by 5 o'clock every morning, including weekends, and within thirty minutes was already poring over material related to the trial.

After a look at the documents, she prepared breakfast for the boys, and by 6:30 when the maid arrived she was ready for a quick look through the newspapers before heading out the door a few minutes later on her way to the courthouse. On most weekdays, she was at her desk or at some other location in the courthouse a few minutes after 7 A.M., already hard at work.

Marcia ultimately lost the skirmish over sealing of the divorce file. In the middle of March, Superior Court Judge Robert Parkin lifted the interim order, and the files were reopened. Judge Parkin continued the previous restriction dating back to July, forbidding release of certain personal information about the children.

The jurist's decision was made after Judy

Forman, one of Marcia's attorneys, cited concerns for her client's sons during a strong argument against making the files available to reporters and the public.

"Those children are not public figures," she declared. "They have a right to not grow up in the limelight."

Gordon's attorney, Roslyn Soudry, asserted in her response that there were no "dire circumstances that would require the documents to be kept secret." Neither of the parents attended the hearing.

Marcia complained in court papers that the press was hounding her so unmercifully she had to change her residence. Reporters were "literally jumping out of the alley," she said.

The prosecutor reported she was barraged by the print and electronic media, including Barbara Walters, *Dateline*, and tabloid television shows seeking interviews. She turned down every request and attempted to keep her private life as private as possible, she said.

Reporters and photographers also began showing up at the Superior Court building for hearings or when other developments were expected on the sensational custody case. Her attorneys in the action were besieged by reporters, pleading for information. One of her lawyers received more than thirty telephone calls from journalists in a single morning.

Indications surfaced in the documents filed by Marcia's estranged husband, indicating she may have helped set the stage for the dismal wrangle when she filed for an increase in financial support. In the petition she cited rising child-care costs and the pressing financial demands of dressing properly for the national television audience.

"I have been working a six- or seven-day week for as many as sixteen hours per day," she declared. "This is probably the most sensational and watched proceeding in the history of the Los Angeles judicial system. . . . I now need baby sitters for the weekends while I work and someone to spend the evenings with my two children."

Marcia cited the huge expense of professional hair care, the cost of the new suits and shoes, and child-care costs she said burgeoned to more than $1,000 a month because of her crushingly long workdays. Because she was a county employee, none of her expenses for her personal care and grooming were reimbursed, she pointed out.

After the couple first broke up, Gordon began paying her $1,100 a month in support. After moving to a larger home, however, he shaved the payments to $650. He claimed that when he said he wanted to spend more time with the boys before Christmas, she warned that she "would have my ass" if he tried to increase his visiting hours.

Gordon said in the court documents he had made the $650-per-month payments since the previous September. He added that he was already in debt at the time she petitioned the court to reinstate the previous larger payments.

The husband balked at paying for her to look good on television, or for what he termed a "Hollywood" makeover.

While she was asking him for more money, he said, she would probably wind up with "astronomical financial windfalls" from the prominent up-front role she was playing in the O. J. trial.

Gordon also argued that the trial was consuming so much of Marcia's time that their sons would be better off living with him. The boys were reputedly starved for affection.

The assertion that Marcia no longer had enough time for the children struck a sore point with many women. The dilemma of working mothers caught between child-care and work responsibilities was a particularly sensitive issue that enflamed passions.

One of the key questions in the minds of many of Marcia's supporters seemed to be:

should a father be able to use a mother's career as an issue in a child custody case?

With her annual salary of $96,829, Marcia earned almost twice as much as her husband. And out of his annual salary of approximately $55,000, the thirty-six-year-old computer engineer was already paying about a third of his after-tax income for support of the boys. He was upset when she petitioned the court for an increase in the payments from him, and said so in court documents.

Prior California court decisions in similar cases strongly opposed discrimination against working mothers in custody matters, because their careers prevented them from spending as much time with the children as they would have liked. They also came down firmly on discrimination against a parent, father or mother, because the other made more money.

Increasing numbers of parents around the country find themselves in court battles over their children and several cases focusing on working mothers have drawn special attention from the media and from advocacy groups. Some of the decisions vary sharply from the trend established in California courts.

One of the most startling and dramatic indications they were firmly in the spotlight, occurred when seven color photographs of

Marcia with her boys were splashed across a two-page center spread in the nationally circulated supermarket tabloid, the *Star*. Looking as if they were snapped by a paparazzi and she was unaware of the intrusion, the exclusive photos showed Marcia at her motherly best. Wearing a dark long-sleeve sweater, she was shown in the largest of the pictures smiling and balancing her purse, another bag, a jacket, and an alphabet board game while she walked alongside Trevor.

The little boy, who also had his hands full, was toddling next to his mother with a pacifier in his mouth. Another photo showed Travis apparently waiting for a hug after greeting his mother as she was getting out of a car. A series of five snapshots showed Travis with his mother and being cuddled.

A lengthy story accompanying the photos that was printed on the two pages and continued on a third, talked about the boys missing their mother because they only saw her about an hour a day. Little Trevor was said to sometimes kiss the television screen when he saw his mother's image there. All in all it provided a touching, heart-warming glimpse of the harried professional mom.

The treatment by the popular supermarket tabloid underscored the hard fact however, that Travis and Trevor could not be shielded as unknown cyphers, no matter how much their parents may have wished that could be true. Because of their mother's deep involvement in the trial, and the angry tussle over custody, they too had become a part of the O. J. Simpson story.

The tempo of the squabble between the Clarks continued to heat up with frightening speed and the unstoppable force of a runaway freight train. It was exceedingly unpleasant, and there was no public indication at least of any possibilities of a cease fire or truce in the foreseeable future.

Some women lined up on the husband's side, and others acknowledged on talk shows or in print that there were two sides to the issue. One prominent feminist pointed out that when the women's movement was launched a quarter of a century ago, one of the early targets for criticism was men who were wedded to their work and didn't spend enough time at the job of parenting.

Now when the same questions were being raised about women workaholics, there was a reluctance by many of those former critics to apply the same standards to their sisters, she pointed out.

While Gordon was doing his desperate best to fend off feminist crusaders and other men and women who were sincerely sympathetic to Marcia, she was deluged under a renewed shower of roses and floral pieces.

Admirers also kept up the barrage of letters, and the entire issue of custody matters and working mothers continued to receive wide play in news columns and on the air waves.

Many of the prosecutor's defenders spoke out with strong assertions that the real consideration should be the quality of Marcia's parenting— not how many hours she worked. But that issue was being sidetracked and somehow lost in the shuffle.

Epilogue

What's Next for Marcia?

So, where does Marcia Clark go from here? What's next up for the feisty, intelligent, and talented woman who has kept the nation entranced for the better part of the past year?

As it has always been, whatever she finally decides to do is up to Marcia. Motherly concern for her sons and other considerations are certain to color and influence her decisions, but ultimately it is her call to make.

The possibilities are dazzling, and are already the subject of widespread speculation in the press and among the millions of trial watchers who have been riveted to their television screens for months observing the complex fascinating woman and her colleagues in their monumental face-off with the O. J. "Dream Team."

Since her presence flared on the public scene, she's been described as everything from "Wonder Woman," a modern-day version of the first century Iceni warrior queen Boadicea who led her people against the Roman invaders in Eastern Britain, the Energizer Bunny, a warm and loving supermom, and on the other side of the coin, as a neglectful workaholic mother who doesn't have enough time for her kids.

Her predicament over the ongoing custody battle with Gordon and the appalling uproar it set off in the press is another matter, but from most indications, she's anxious to put the entire sordid mess to rest as soon as she can so that both she and the children can regain a modicum of privacy. She's always made it plain she wants the boys kept out of the public eye.

She is universally respected in her chosen profession. If she wished to, she could probably leave the District Attorney's Office as so many other talented and successful prosecutors have previously done in jurisdictions throughout the country and put her energies and talents to use as a criminal defense attorney.

A spirited bidding war would probably break out among prestigious Los Angeles area law firms if she indicated she was available as a recruit. Not only her impressive legal talents, but the glamor and celebrity attained as the O. J. prosecutor and television star would carry definite dollar appeal.

At this moment, if you were in serious trouble with the law, Marcia Clark was available, and you could afford her, who would you pick to defend you in court?

Marcia could also become a hot property in Tinseltown. She's had limited training as an actress and has danced professionally. Importantly, she has also proven to millions of people that she can handle herself well on camera and say all of her lines correctly without hemming and hawing or interrupting with a bunch of distracting "um, uh's," or irritating "you knows."

Furthermore, she's already a proven star. The national exposure and fallout flare and sizzle from the trial has already worked wonders for others with Hollywood dreams who have played far less visible roles in the grotesque prime-time tragedy.

But if anyone knows for sure what her career decision will be after all the briefs, pleadings, and evidence are gathered up, the courtroom bombast and shadow boxing with the truth is over, witnesses and jurors have returned to their jobs and homes, and lawbooks are closed on the blockbuster trial that's still underway in Courtroom 103— it's Marcia herself.

Marcia Clark:

A Chronology

August 31, 1953. Born in Berkeley, California, to Abraham I. and Rozlyn Mazur Kleks.

1972. Receives graduation diploma from Susan Wagner High School on Staten Island, N. Y.

1973. Student at UCLA when she moves in to live with Israeli Air Force veteran and professional backgammon player Gabriel G. Horowitz.

1976. Graduates from UCLA with her undergraduate degree in political science.

1976. Married to Gabriel on November 6.

1979. Earns her law degree from Southwestern University School of Law in Los Angeles. Passes California Bar examination, and begins work specializing in criminal law as a junior attorney with Brodey and Price, a Los Angeles firm.

1980. Files in Los Angeles for divorce from Gabriel, citing "Irreconcilable differences" in July.

1980. Drives to Tijuana and obtains a Mexican divorce in September.

1980. Married to Gordon Tolls Clark, a Scientologist and computer expert, on October 7. Her maiden name, "Kleks" was used on the marriage license.

1981. American divorce is finalized in the Los Angeles county courts on February 2.

Hired by Los Angeles District Attorney John Van De Kamp, as an Assistant District Attorney, and begins prosecuting homicide cases at the courthouse in Culver City. She holds other assignments, including in the Training and the Juvenile Divisions.

1985. Assigned to work with Harvey Giss on the high-profile James Hawkins murder trial, and together they win double-murder convictions against the one-time Watts folk hero. The trial, when she worked side by side with the man considered to be the D.A.'s top gun in homicide prosecutions, marks Marcia's move into the trial lawyer Big Leagues.

1989. Her first child, Travis Clark, is born.

1992. Second son, Trevor Clark, is born.

1994. Marcia and Gordon break up and

he moves out of their house early in the new year.

June 9, 1994. Marcia files in Los Angeles Superior Court for divorce from Gordon, her husband of nearly thirteen years.

June 13, 1994. Marcia is assigned to assist police in preparation of search warrants and other aspects of the investigation into the slayings of Nicole Brown Simpson and Ronald Goldman. The assignment quickly leads to her permanent appointment as one of the two lead prosecutors in the case.

INFORMATIVE —
COMPELLING —
SCINTILLATING —
NON-FICTION FROM PINNACLE TELLS THE TRUTH!

BORN TOO SOON (751, $4.50)
by Elizabeth Mehren

This is the poignant story of Elizabeth's daughter Emily's premature birth. As the parents of one of the 275,000 babies born prematurely each year in this country, she and her husband were plunged into the world of the Neonatal Intensive Care unit. With stunning candor, Elizabeth Mehren relates her gripping story of unshakable faith and hope — and of courage that comes in tiny little packages.

THE PROSTATE PROBLEM (745, $4.50)
by Chet Cunningham

An essential, easy-to-use guide to the treatment and prevention of the illness that's in the headlines. This book explains in clear, practical terms all the facts. Complete with a glossary of medical terms, and a comprehensive list of health organizations and support groups, this illustrated handbook will help men combat prostate disorder and lead longer, healthier lives.

THE ACADEMY AWARDS HANDBOOK (887, $4.50)

An interesting and easy-to-use guide for movie fans everywhere, the book features a year-to-year listing of all the Oscar nominations in every category, all the winners, an expert analysis of who wins and why, a complete index to get information quickly, and even a 99% foolproof method to pick this year's winners!

WHAT WAS HOT (894, $4.50)
by Julian Biddle

Journey through 40 years of the trends and fads, famous and infamous figures, and momentous milestones in American history. From hoola hoops to rap music, greasers to yuppies, Elvis to Madonna — it's all here, trivia for all ages. An entertaining and evocative overview of the milestones in America from the 1950's to the 1990's!